POWER
FOR
EVERYDAY
HEROES

Inspiration and Strength for Men

Compiled by
John and Crystal Earnhardt

Pacific Press Publishing Association
Boise, Idaho
Oshawa, Ontario, Canada

Edited by Kenneth R. Wade
Designed by Dennis Ferree
Typeset in 12.5/16 Esprit

ISBN 0-8163-1299-0

96 97 98 99 00 • 5 4 3 2 1

Stories, devotionals, and personal experiences—Jesus used them to teach important lessons. And so have the authors of this book—with the goal of uplifting Jesus. The authors' share of the proceeds from the sale of the book will go directly to aid with Global Mission projects around the world in the hope that the work of evangelism will soon be finished and we can all go home to be with our heavenly Father.

This book has been written by men from various walks of life, occupations, and cultures. Each writer has volunteered to share his wisdom, wit, experiences—and most important of all—his faith in Jesus Christ.

Contents

Introduction

"No man is an island. No man stands alone." My fourth-grade music teacher taught us that song for a special school function. The words didn't make much sense to me then. Of course, a man isn't an island—but some men do stand alone. My nine-year-old mind didn't understand the reasoning of an adult.

I never really thought about that song again until one crisp autumn day when I saw a flock of geese flying in a V formation. Grandfather saw me observing them and took the opportunity to teach me a valuable lesson. "Did you know that geese can fly farther than eagles?" he asked.

"No. How can they? An eagle is bigger and stronger."

"A goose is a big bird too, but if he were to fight an eagle, I have no doubt that the eagle would win," Grandpa agreed. "But nevertheless, geese can fly farther than eagles." He leaned forward, indicating that some marvelous tidbit of wisdom was forthcoming. And I wasn't disappointed.

"The geese have a secret."

"What is it, Grandpa?"

"They never fly alone. Well," he added, "at least when they decide to go on a long journey, they fly in groups. You see that one at the tip of the V? His outstretched neck is like a spear slicing the wind or breaking the air. That causes an upward wind that lifts the birds behind. The others don't have to flap so hard. They're kind of riding on a draft. When the lead bird gets tired, he or she simply drops back, and another bird takes the lead. Not one of them insists on being the leader all the time. They take turns and share in the work, soaring on each other's strength.

"It wouldn't hurt us to learn a lesson from those geese," Grandpa went on to say. "We need each other. One man might have knowledge in the brain but be as puny as a kitten. Another might be strong as an ox but have bats in his belfry. If the two work together and use each other's strengths, they can get something accomplished."

I've never forgotten Grandpa's observation. So that's what the song meant. We need each other. Few were meant to soar alone, solitary and self-sufficient. That's why the apostle Paul likened the people in the church to different parts of the body. Each one is given different spiritual gifts. You may be supportive like the feet or powerful like an arm, but you're not greater or more important than a toe or a finger.

The following pages are filled with testimonies and wisdom from men with a variety of gifts, fulfilling various roles. Men who have been there. Ministers, businessmen, blue-collar workers, doctors, and educators. They have volunteered their labor in the hope that their words may help others on their flight through life.

Section 1 is devoted to our heavenly Father—His character, sacrifice, and invitation to meet Him at Calvary. Respected ministers like Ron Halvorsen and Mark Finley offer a unique perspective of the cross.

Section 2 is a collection of memorable art-of-living experiences. Men share adventures and exciting testimonies that just may change your life.

Section 3 deals with overcoming our number-one enemy, the devil. One man's interaction with a predator yields deep insights into how to avoid Satan's traps. Another man's encounter with a bear teaches a valuable lesson.

Section 4 is written by men who share how to bring God into your business life. They offer wisdom for dealing with the tools of trade.

Section 5 discusses relationships, marriage, and children.

Section 6 is devoted to character development and self-help. Professionals write about self-esteem, the power of sensitivity, and the stewardship of power.

Section 1

We Call Him Father

*As a father has compassion
on his children,
so the Lord has compassion
on those who fear him.*

———————

Psalms 103:13, NIV.

"When he was yet a great way off, his father saw him, and had compassion, and ran, and fell on his neck, and kissed him." Luke 15:20.

———

Daddy, What Is God Like?

by Ron Halvorsen

It was one of those rare moments in the life of a preacher. It was late in the evening, and I was seated on one of those space-age recliners. The kind you can stretch out in, push a button, and it shakes you a little, push another button, and it warms you up. My son Ronnie sat on my lap while I read bedtime stories. He interrupted every other sentence with questions that only a four-year-old can think of. But one of his questions was so profound that it arrested my mind. "Daddy, what is God like?"

"Well, He's like a . . ." I stroked my chin as he looked into my face.

"Well, He's umm, umm . . ."

How do you explain that to a four-year-old? I've had difficult, diligent questions before, asked by men of great intellect, but this one seemed more important than the others.

POWER FOR EVERYDAY HEROES

One cannot think very far into the tangled world situations, as we view them with our eyes and heart, without asking questions about God. What is God like? Or closer still, how does God feel? How does God feel when He hears in the world the thunder of guns as people hunt each other down on land and sea? How does God feel when He sees terrorists kill a man in a wheelchair and throw him overboard to get the attention of the world? How does He feel when He sees this lovely planet defaced by strife, lust, human woe, and passion? Not alone on the battlefield, not alone in the problems of life, but what is God like in the hospital room or the funeral home? This is the big question behind all questions, and until it is answered, there can be no believing. Sometimes it is asked anxiously and sometimes, asked in bewilderment. But people are crying out, "God, what are You like?"

In the Old Testament, He is called "the Judge," "God Almighty," or "Jehovah," but the great word on the lips of Jesus Christ is *Father*. The rallying catchword of the Gospels is *Father*. From His earliest years, "I must be about my Father's business" to "Our Father which art in heaven," right down to the end, when He hung on the cross, "Father, why hast thou forsaken me?" Always first and last, *Father*—a name so rich in tenderness.

He took that name and wove it into a story so meaningful, so contemporary and dynamic—the story of the prodigal son. It's not just about a young man who wants to leave home; it's really about the waiting father. It's not about a boy who wastes his inheritance in riotous living or winds up in a pigpen—nor is it a story of a reckless, loose life. It's the story of God and how He seeks and saves. The tender, patient love and devotion of a father. The kind of father who sorrows over our estrangement and separation from Him.

All parents feel loneliness to a degree when they bring a child into the world and love that child with all their heart, only to see that child grow up and find satisfaction, enjoyment, and companionship outside of home. Or to see that child grow coarse and fling away their birthright like a fool. Or to wish the best for their child and see them choose the worst.

God also sorrows over our poverty. That young man left home, vibrant and healthy, with a great dream. He came back looking old, shattered, and weak. There is poverty outside of the Father's house. We are poor because of our choices.

When the son was a great way off, the father saw him. God is never nearsighted. He is a father who waits, watches, and runs. He seeks and pursues us.

There are times in my life when I need to hear the footsteps of God running toward me. He who could crush us stoops to redeem us. While we look for justice, God looks for mercy.

My father was an alcoholic until Jesus came into his life. But he had many good traits about him. I'll never forget that Christmas so long ago. Father was out of work, and we heard him tell Mother that there would be no Christmas presents that year. Even boys who live in tenements look forward to Christmas.

But then one night he came home with a gleam in his eyes.

We heard him tell Mother that he was going to make Christmas. He placed a sign on the door of a big room that we shut off in the winter. It read "Santa's Workshop." Every night he would come home and go behind that closed door. My father was a pipe fitter, not a carpenter. Yet we heard him hammering and sawing until the wee hours of the morning.

Finally, Christmas Eve arrived. All five of us boys went to bed early. The next morning, we saw the most beautiful tree ever. It was just a scrawny tree that some store owner had thrown out, but under that tree were five packages wrapped in newspaper. We scrambled to them. I will never forget my present. A little homemade red wagon. Dad had taken an orange crate and painted it and attached four of the crookedest wheels you can imagine. But I was so proud of that wagon. Why? Because my father hammered into it his love.

"Daddy, what is God like?"

"Well, son, he's like a father."

Ron Halvorsen has traveled around the world and won thousands of people to the Lord during his evangelistic ministry. He is now serving as evangelism coordinator in the Southern Union.

For each of these three men, the deciding factor was the cross.
One carried the cross.
One died on a cross.
One nailed the Saviour to a cross.

———

Three Men Meet Jesus

by Mark A. Finley

On the darkest Friday in all history, three men meet Jesus. The first meets Him as He struggles—stumbling beneath the weight of an enormous cross—along the path to the mount called Calvary. When Jesus falls to the path in exhaustion, His cross is placed on the brawny shoulders of this man.

A second man meets Jesus while hanging at His side on a cross of his own. But before breathing his last, he finds new hope and life in the Saviour's assurance of salvation.

The third meets Jesus while standing in Roman armor at the foot of the cross. As he witnesses Christ's dying agonies and hears His words of forgiveness, the stern heart of the centurion is broken, and he cries out in conviction, "This man is the Son of God!"

These three men came from widely diverse backgrounds. Their life experiences—and their ways of viewing things—

were certainly not the same. Yet they shared one thing in common: When each met Jesus, he was never the same again.

Join me in considering these three:

1. Simon, a hard-working African farmer—the compelled one.
2. The thief, a rebellious Judean youth—the crucified one.
3. The Roman centurion, a hardened military officer—the callous one.

Simon: the compelled one

The Scriptures describe Simon in one brief text: "As they came out, they found a man of Cyrene, Simon by name: him they compelled to bear his cross" (Matthew 27:32, KJV).

To compel is to forcibly press someone into service. The word in the original language is a military term meaning "to commandeer"—it implies a strict order. He was *drafted*—conscripted into service. He has no choice in the matter. He was forced—coerced.

Picture the scene. He has arrived after a long, arduous journey to Palestine. He rounds a sharp corner on a narrow cobblestone Jerusalem street and finds himself face to face with a jeering mob. He is swept up in the crowd and carried along as if by a wave of the sea. The Roman soldiers force the Son of God through the mass of shouting people. Weary, suffering, weak from the loss of blood following two Roman lashings, Jesus falls in exhaustion at Simon's feet. He can no longer go on.

It doesn't seem fair that Simon should have been forced to carry a cross that was not even his own—that he should have been rudely detained from whatever mission had brought him to Jerusalem, to assist in an execution. For Simon, what happened that day was not fair. Yet in that cross he found his life's greatest blessing. The cross was the means of his salvation, the source of his reconciliation to his Creator.

Some of us today, like Simon, are conscripted and compelled to carry crosses not of our choosing. Loss of a job, marital problems, straying children, or other sudden events thrust circumstances upon us as a cross. The demands seem too heavy, the load too great. Yet, as someone has said:

> "Every trial is a call to prayer,
> Every burden a bridge to the Saviour,
> Every difficulty an invitation to our knees."

Three men met Jesus: Simon, the compelled one, met Him under the crushing load of a heavy burden. Perhaps that is where you, too, will meet Him.

The penitent thief: the crucified one

The second man to meet Jesus that day was the thief dying on the cross. Evidently he was a companion of Barabbas, who claimed to be the Messiah. This young man dying on the cross had accepted an illusion; he had grasped at a phantom. He was a Jew for whom religion didn't satisfy, who sought freedom but came up empty-handed. He was a seeker who sought answers in all the wrong places. He had probably heard Jesus preach. But his careless attitude toward religion led him to compromise.

The thief had no doubt been brought up in a conservative Jewish home. He attended rabbinical schools; he kept the Sabbath and meticulously followed laws of health. But his religion was only an external form. And his cynical attitude toward religion led him to pursue his own selfish interests where the law stood as a challenge.

Soon the long arm of Roman law reached for him. He was arrested, jailed, tried, found guilty, and condemned to death. And now he was being executed. There was no escape.

As blood dripped from those nail wounds, he couldn't pull his hands or legs free and walk away. This was for real. The stench of death was in the air. He couldn't move, because it hurt too much. Suddenly, it dawned upon him—he was going to die!

Guilt—a gnawing inner discomfort, a sense of being off balance, a sense that everything was not right between himself and God—seized his entire being.

In those final moments, the penitent thief cried out, "Lord, remember me!" Never has that plea gone unanswered. There in those last moments, amidst his suffering, peace flooded into his soul. His sins were forgiven. Beyond the pain, he had the assurance of heaven at last.

Three men meet Jesus: one meets Him ascending a hill. Another meets Him hanging by His side. Still another meets Him standing at His feet. All meet Him and are changed.

Three Men Meet Jesus

The Roman centurion: the callous one

It was a violent age, in a violent land, among a violent people—and he was a violent man. The Roman soldier was a hardhearted, callous, rough, tough fighter. He was a soldier of fortune, always on guard for the unexpected ambush. He handled people roughly. He was truly an unlikely prospect for the gospel. As superintendent of executions and a professional killer of criminals, his heart was hardened against any religious thought.

The Scriptures call him a centurion—the commander of one hundred men. He was amazed that Jesus offered no resistance. Christ's suffering only revealed His kingly glory. He submitted to the nails without flinching; He lay down without a struggle. As the cross was lifted and plunged with great violence into the hole prepared for it, no cursing proceeded from His lips—only a prayer. "Father, forgive them."

As he watched Jesus' loving disposition toward His enemies, the centurion exclaimed, "Truly, this was the Son of God." The centurion may have recalled Pilate's judgment hall. Jesus was mighty in weakness. His cross was a throne—His thorns the crown of the universe.

There at the cross, the centurion laid down his sword and shield. There on Golgotha's hill, he laid down his weapons. Jesus took that cruel, callous, unfeeling Roman officer and changed him into another man.

Can you think of three more seemingly hopeless cases?

1. A stranger from Africa.
2. A thief condemned to death—an inmate on death row.

3. An officer in the Roman army whose callous heart made him eligible for the post of superintendent of executions.

Like the centurion, I crucify my Saviour and put Him to open shame. At the cross, I lay my weapons down, committing my life to Him. Like the thief, I die with Jesus. ("I am crucified with Christ"; see Galatians 2:20.) At the cross, I receive forgiveness. Like Simon, I must take up my cross, daily. I cheerfully bear the burdens Christ allows to come my way.

Will you join me at the cross?

Mark Finley is the speaker and director of *It Is Written*. Reprinted with permission from the book *Final Days*, by Mark Finley.

He was growing older and should have been enjoying his retirement. But something held him back. A story of a father's self-sacrificing love that will touch your heart.

———

Just in Case

by Charles Mills

I sat on the steps watching my father chop logs into firewood. His steady hand and quick reflexes reassured me he was still in good health, even into his retirement years.

Seeing my parents grow older unnerved me a bit. For some reason, I'd expected them to live forever, to be young and energetic indefinitely. But sin had carved the path of aging long ago, and my mom and dad were simply traveling an-all-too- familiar road through life. I still didn't like it.

"You can take these to the porch," Dad said, pointing at the pile of freshly split wood. "I'll start working on a new stack."

I gathered an armful of the dry oak for my first trip to the wood bin. Walking around the side of the house, I admired its homey contours and tree-filled surroundings. This was a great place to retire.

"Why are you doing this?" I asked, returning for another load.

"Doing what?" The ax split a log with a resounding crack.

"Why are you working so hard to chop all this wood? It's not like you need to. After all, you have a perfectly good furnace in the basement; your retirement benefits pay the bills; the house and car are yours free and clear. Surely you can afford heating oil."

"That's true," he said, running the back of his hand across his forehead. "But you never know. Could be one of you kids might need a little help down the road."

"We're all gainfully employed for the present," I argued. "Come on, Dad; live a little. Don't work so hard."

He placed another log on the block and took careful aim. "I know," he said as the wood fractured. "But something might come up. It's nice to have a little set aside for you guys just in case."

My father was cutting wood he didn't have to cut. He was working hard to save money he didn't have to save, to help a child who didn't need any help.

My mother and father had always provided for us kids. No, we were never considered wealthy. My dad's forty-three years of church employment had allowed little money for the bank, although we were always rich in love and affection. Having four children in church school and college at the same time hadn't helped either. Now, when they could occasionally set aside a few cents, they were still putting our needs first.

Dad was chopping wood "just in case."

My heavenly Father understands that practice too. He knew there would be those who might need Him, so He left the courts of glory, just in case.

He was born as a babe, just in case a child cried out in the night needing comfort. He grew up under the watchcare of human parents, just in case a lonely boy or girl needed a father's care. He walked among the poor and sick, just in case there was a hurting heart or mind longing to feel His presence. He studied the religious teachings of the world, just in case a pastor or priest needed answers to heart-troubling questions. He slept in the arms of the elements, just in case a downcast voice moaned its despair from a park bench or cold, hard sidewalk.

He allowed Himself to be sold for thirty pieces of silver, just in case a soul in slavery longed to be free. He felt the sharp pain of the whip, just in case a whimper arose from a prison cell. He stood unspeaking before lying witnesses, just in case a child of God was accused unjustly. And in that awful hour, the Creator of the universe died the agonizing death of a sinner, just in case there was a soul to save.

I stood and watched my father chopping wood. And suddenly, I felt the power of that love on reserve for me in heaven, just in case I need it.

Charles Mills is the owner of Christian Communications in Berkeley Springs, West Virginia. He has written numerous books and articles.

*Treasure the gift of a father's love
in this moving reminiscence of events
that happened during the Depression.*

The Warmth
of His Presence

by Jan Doward

Recalling memories of my father invariably triggers a host of warm sensory impressions of total loving comfort and assurance and peace.

I can still remember him bringing a brick heated in the oven and wrapped in a towel into my bedroom on cold nights when I was a small lad. Slipping it under the covers by my feet, he would then give me a squeeze and tuck me in for the night.

When I was about nine, we rented a house near a place where some burglars had lived. I didn't think much about it during the daytime, but after dark, my mind raced with all sorts of scary thoughts. Whoever they were just might show up on the balcony right off my back bedroom! Such thoughts only made me curl up under the covers until it got so stuffy I just had to get my head out for air. That was when the thirst ritual would kick in. Knowing my parents' bedroom was on the other side of the wall by my head, I'd call loudly.

The Warmth of His Presence

"Daddy, I wanna drink of water!"

No matter how tired he was, Dad would always come, pick me up, and carry me in his arms to the sink, where I would get a drink. I never drank more than a sip or two that I can remember, but how I loved the reassurance of his presence! I could always go right to sleep after that.

About the time I was in the sixth grade, we moved for the last time. Now Dad had a little shop near our house where he could rewind electrical motors in the evenings. The Depression years had dragged on a lot longer than anyone expected, and it seemed that Dad had to work early and late. Although he held a job at the Cascade Electrical and Machinery Company in south Seattle, which took an hour's drive one way, Dad would go to his home shop as a "second shift" after supper. I liked to go out there with him. To be truthful, I was never as interested in what he was doing so much as I liked being with him. I enjoyed watching him smile, seeing the corners of his eyes wrinkle, and hearing him laugh. Dad had a very shoppy odor about him, too, that made me feel good inside. I would sit on a high stool next to his work bench and just absorb his presence.

During those years, Dad didn't have much time for vacations except on weekends. We had been poor so long it seemed he wanted to catch up to the place where there would not be so much month at the end of the money. Once, during that time, he set aside a day when just the two of us could be alone. What to do? Immediately, I chose to spend the whole day at a hidden beach on Puget Sound called "Lost World." I had already discovered a steep, narrow trail through deep woods to the beach, and for a long time I had wanted Dad to see this special beach.

When the day arrived, however, the rain poured from dark gray skies in a typical Northwest drenching. I would well understand if Dad wanted to postpone the venture. Instead, he smiled at me that morning.

"Let's go anyway!"

We put on our rain gear, took sufficient newspaper and matches along with an old tarp, and hiked to "Lost World." We built a little lean-to out of driftwood, draped the tarp over the top for a roof, and hunkered down over a fire Dad had built. I can't remember a thing we talked about that day or anything else we did except watch the rain and tide, but the memory of being by his side all day still generates a warm joy in my heart. The strength of his character and personality lingers with a fondness that simply will not go away.

I have often thought about Dad when reading Psalm 16:11: "Thou wilt shew me the path of life: in thy presence is fulness of joy; at thy right hand there are pleasures for evermore." So often we seem to think we have to be going and doing for pleasure, but for those who understand the sheer joy of God's presence, nothing in this world compares to it. Worshipfully absorbing His presence through His Word and the things He has made assures us of the most profound joy possible. Heaven itself comes very near to those who have discovered the secret of this fullness of joy.

Jan S. Doward is a retired teacher, youth leader, and pastor. He has written for various publications. *Footsteps of an Approaching God* is one of the many books he has written.

*When four weeks of raw sewage accidently flood the
church basement, one man gleans a spiritual lesson
from the most embarrassing moment of his life.*

———

Cleaning Up Our Mess

by Gary D. Gibbs

For several years, my wife and I called a thirty-five-foot,
fifth-wheel travel trailer "home." We were newlyweds,
inexperienced in trailer living, and I was an evangelist. We
were just at the end of a tiring four-week evangelistic series
in the rolling mountains of the Northeast. It was to be our
last evening meeting. Since our next series of meetings was
to begin in a few days and we still had several states to cross,
we were very busy that last Friday getting the trailer ready
to pull out the first thing Sunday morning. To make matters worse, a snowstorm was in the forecast, which meant
I had to get off the mountain where we were parked, if I was
to have any hope of getting to my next destination on time.
But there was one undesirable piece of business that still
remained to be taken care of.

Normally, we connected the trailer directly to the city
sewer wherever we were parked. But during this particu-

lar meeting, our trailer was precariously balanced on the side of a mountain that sloped steeply down to a large river. The spot was so steep that the rear end of the trailer kissed the dirt while the front end towered nearly six feet above ground. This, coupled with the long run we had on the sewer hose, kept the sewer from properly emptying for the entire month. Four weeks of raw sewage in the trailer's holding tanks patiently waited to be emptied before I could travel.

Since we were unable to locate a sewer dump, the pastor and I decided to dump it in the sewer lines in the basement of the church. I connected the sewer hose to my trailer. Then I carefully ran the flexible hose through the basement window to the pastor. He put the hose in the church's sewer line. The plan was for me to wait until he gave me the word, and then I would open the valve on the trailer.

Shortly, I heard the pastor shout from the basement, "OK, let her go." With that, I pulled the plug. Four weeks of raw sewage went rushing through the hose like a raging flash flood down a canyon. Because the trailer was at a higher level than the basement, the flow was terribly strong. In fact, the current was so forceful that it knocked the hose out of the pastor's hands, thereby causing the end to slip out of the church sewer line. I couldn't see what was happening, but I certainly could hear the pastor crying, "No! No! Stop! Stop!" Quickly, I shut off the valve. But it was too late. The church basement was flooded with the most foul material known to humankind.

This was God's house, and I was the guest evangelist. What a predicament! Worst of all, the final evangelistic meeting was only two hours away, and the stench was quickly wafting upstairs and filling the sanctuary. We had to act fast.

I volunteered to clean up the basement, but no matter how much I protested, the pastor insisted on doing it himself. I can't tell you how humbling it was to have this dear friend and colleague clean up my nasty sewage. He mopped up bucket after bucket while I aired out the sanctuary and sprayed a can of deodorizer. Fortunately, when the people arrived two hours later, they never knew what had happened.

Embarrassing as this incident was, it proved to be one of those magic moments when God turns calamity into a blessing. "All things work together for good," the Bible promises (see Romans 8:28). And in this experience, I discovered the promise to be true. What is most riveted in my mind about an event that I would otherwise like to forget is the picture of Jesus, and what it means to be a man of God that the pastor gave me that day.

You see, the pure, spotless Son of God left His holy throne in heaven and came to this wretched world, defiled and polluted by sin. With His sacrificial life and death, He humbled Himself to mop up the sewage of my sins. Imagine how repulsive sin must have been to His sinless character! But because He loves us so much, He insisted on cleaning up our sins. And He still cleans up our sin each and every day. There is never a complaint from Him. He is willing and ready to share His love with sinners such as us.

Gary Gibbs is an ordained minister and evangelist who helps churches to prepare for evangelistic meetings.

33

Section 2

Life's Valuable Lessons

Blessed is the man
who does not walk in the counsel of the wicked
or stand in the way of sinners
or sit in the seat of mockers.
But his delight is in the law of the LORD,
and on his law he meditates day and night.
He is like a tree planted by streams of water,
which yields its fruit in season
and whose leaf does not wither.
Whatever he does prospers.

Psalms 1:1-3.

Before the race began, a few fans held up a banner that read,
"If God was a stock car racer
His name would be Earnhardt."

———

Road to
Glory

by John Earnhardt

It is the Coca-Cola 600, Memorial Day Weekend. A crowd of more than 162,000 gathers in Concord, North Carolina, at the Charlotte Motor Speedway. For the first time, the 600-mile stock-car race will begin in midafternoon and end under artificial lighting.

Dale Earnhardt has been in front for sixty-four laps—fending off challenges from Irvan, Elliott, and Allison—when he pits after 220 laps and is penalized for speeding in pit row. The crowd boos while Earnhardt loses valuable time.

Meanwhile, Jarrett and Irvan feel the tension building. If either of them wins this race and the next, they have a shot at one million dollars. But Earnhardt is determined to catch up and finds himself behind Greg Sax, unable to get around. Suddenly, the calm sportscaster's voice shouts.

"Oh! Greg Sax is getting tagged. He comes right in front

of car number 3! Moving by is car number 4! Earnhardt brings out a caution!"

Greg Sax spins sideways off the track, forcing Earnhardt to put on the brakes to avoid hitting him. The TV replays those few seconds over and over, trying to see if Dale Earnhardt purposely tagged Sax in the rear. Earnhardt swears he never touched him but is penalized one lap for rough driving anyway. Says the sportscaster, "It's like sticking your hand in a beehive. Dale is irate."

Plainly infuriated, Dale is determined to show the world what he's made of. He puts the pedal to the metal, and minutes later, the sportscasters are shouting again. "What a battle for the lead! Earnhardt and Ernie Irvan are wheel to wheel! And Earnhardt goes back in front! ... Right down the pass! . . . Ducked to the inside!"

At twenty-five laps to go, there were nine cars on the lead lap. Forty-one drivers started the race. Now only twenty-nine remain. There have been ten different leaders and twenty-nine lead changes.

I sit in my Lazyboy recliner and watch while Dale Earnhardt flies by the white flag, savoring his third 600 win and his fifty-fifth victory. Now $156,650 richer and boosting his U.S. auto-racing record past $17 million.

He cruises down victory lane, taking time to wave to his fans. Then as the car comes to a stop in the winner's circle, he wipes the sweat off his face, takes a quick drink of Gatorade, and emerges out of car number 3 while fireworks go off behind him and an army of newscasters swarms in front of him. His victory is sweet, and he savors his win in spite of the penalties.

I smile and sit back, my mind drifting down the corridors of time to another race, another era, when racing was a sport and not a full-time profession.

We were little then, Dale and I. Two skinny, barefoot kids who played on the dusty sides of the infield until the loudspeakers announced the lineup. My dad owned a race-track about a quarter of a mile through the woods behind our house. He raced micro midget cars. Dale's father, Ralph Earnhardt, would later become a professional stock car driver. He didn't spend much time with micro midgets, but he did spend many a Sunday afternoon at our track cheering on his friends.

I'd stand as close to the track as my mom would allow and hold my breath while the command rang out, "Gentlemen, start your engines." The cars would slowly circle the track in perfect formation, two cars side by side in the lineup. No one dared blink an eye until after the momentous second when the green flag was lowered and the cars roared off. The rest was a blur of spinning wheels; sweaty, shouting fans; hot dogs; and caution flags.

Dale and I are only one year apart in age. We grew up in the same general area. Both of our fathers were entranced with speed and the thrill of flying past that checkered flag before all the others. We shared the same last name, though neither of us has checked to see where we stand in the line of genes. Both of us are approximately the same height and build. Our noses are shaped the same (with pores a little too large for my taste) and blue eyes set back in our heads. Our hairlines are even receding in the same places.

Yet in spite of these similarities, our worlds are far apart.

Fame and glory have claimed Dale Earnhardt. His name has made the headlines in every newspaper in the United States and many other countries besides. We started down the same highway, but somewhere along the way, our roads veered off in opposite directions.

While he decided to follow in his father's blaze of glory, I embarked on another kind of race. This race requires all the wisdom, skill, and endurance that I can develop. I, too, learn from my Father. He watches over me day by day, giving instructions and cheering me on. But unlike stock car races, all who make it to the finish line will receive a trophy and a crown.

"Seeing we also are compassed about with so great a cloud of witnesses, let us lay aside every weight, and the sin which doth so easily beset us, and let us run with patience the race that is set before us" (Hebrews 12:1, KJV).

John Earnhardt has been a pastor in Maryland and North Carolina and an evangelist for *Amazing Facts*. He is currently pastoring in North Carolina.

Is there a reason behind sports mania?
A humorous observation behind one man's
athletic adventures that resulted in . . .

———

Sporting Significance

by Karl Haffner

I love sports. Where else do you get a chance to boo a whole slew of millionaires to their faces?

I not only love to watch sports, I love to play. Unfortunately, I'm as coordinated as a moose on ice skates. My skills notwithstanding, I've dabbled in almost every sport from skiing to parasailing.

Skiing

Skiing looked easy. At least, my cousin Danny made it sound easy. "All you've got to do," he said, "is strap these waxed boards to your feet and point the tips down the mountain."

He took me to Mount Snow—that resort world famous all over the town of Newfane, Vermont. Danny noticed my fear and comforted me, "Don't worry; anybody with an IQ higher than a jar of mustard can ski."

I figured I could at least get up the mountain. I shuffled toward the lift line with the confidence of a mouse at a cat convention. The line moved forward—but not as fast as I did. Are you familiar with the Domino theory? Fifty skiers came tumbling down. So nobody would know who caused the pileup, I peeped from the bottom, "Who fell?"

Getting off the ski lift wasn't much easier. How was I to know I was supposed to get off before the chair curled around to head back down the hill? (I guess that's where the IQ/mustard test comes in.) Unfortunately, an astute lift attendant noticed I was safely heading down the mountain and alertly stopped the chairs and commanded me: "Jump."

"Jump?" I echoed in disbelief. I slid to the edge of my seat. Closing my eyes, I lunged forward and dropped like a shot duck. I landed in front of a sign displaying a large black diamond with the name of the run: The Devil's Vomit. I peered over the edge like a cat wanting down from the roof of the Trump Tower. The ski lodge looked five states away.

Three hours later, I was thirty feet down the mountain—only because I was wearing slippery clothing. Eventually, I did make it to the bottom, but not gracefully. Are you familiar with the snowball theory? I rolled down the mountain like an avalanche. My shrieks alerted the ninety-nine skiers in my way that unless they wanted to take their next run in a wheelchair, they had best stay clear.

As I was bombing toward the ski lodge at Mach 2, a minor question crept into my head: How does one stop? Then I discovered the reasons for trees along ski runs. I concluded skiing is not my spiritual gift, so I thought I'd give an easier sport a shot: parasailing.

Parasailing

"You parasail ever?" the man asked in broken English.

"No," I quipped as he strapped me into a contraption that looked like the skeleton of a full-body diaper. "But it doesn't look too hard."

"When boat goes, you . . ." the Mexican rambled in a language I barely understood.

My mind drifted as I gazed at the white beaches of Acapulco. "Now, señor, red flag vairdy, vairdy important, means . . ."

I flinched a bit as he tightened the strap against my sunburn.

"And dis white flag when I wave is . . ."

I breathed deeply, savoring the salty aroma.

"Dat's it," the Mexican screamed to the boat driver as I was whisked off my feet.

Faster than I could say "adios, amigos," I was floating three hundred feet above the water. "Yeeeeehaaaaaw," I yelled. I was having more fun than a flea at a dog show. Until the landing.

As the boat circled around, I descended toward the guy who was frantically waving his red flag. I struggled to remember what he had said about that flag. Although I could vaguely recall him saying it was "vairdy important," I couldn't remember what it meant.

I was plummeting toward a beach hut ("Dagaberto's Delicious Drinks"). I crashed into it with the force of a refrigerator ("William Perry"), smashing margaritas and piña coladas that instantly belonged to me ($67.83). Fortunately, besides a scolding ("You-never-parasail-here-again!"), all I got was a bruise larger than my skin surface area.

Oh yeah, I also got a chance to ask myself again, Why would a klutz like me bother with sports anyway? What drives men to sports?

Why bother?

I'm still a lousy athlete who won't retire the cleats. I continue to uphold the value of sports. Research indicates that participating in sports activities reduces stress, which in turn reduces the likelihood of divorce. Amazingly, the statistics hold true for spectator sports: Divorce rates in cities with Major League baseball teams are 25 percent lower than in cities without teams! Sports can be worthwhile.

Dr. Willard Harley, in his book *His Needs, Her Needs*, contends that recreation is a great need for men—second only to sexual fulfillment. After thirty years of research and counseling, he argues that most men have a real need for sports and recreation. Our obsession with sports reflects a deeper need.

Early in my ministry, I made an observation that still baffles me: Why is it that some men drag in late to our third worship service at 12:30 p.m., yet have no problem showing up Sunday mornings at 7:30 sharp to play football? Why the obsession with sports?

I suspect that the deeper force fueling this obsession is the need within every man to feel significant. To make a difference at the buzzer. To revel in the admiration of onlookers. To be part of a team. To excel. To win.

While sports can have value in a Christians's life, no athletic achievement will satisfy this deeper need. The difference in men is in how we try to fulfill this more profound quest to feel significant. Some serve the soccer god. Others the god of skiing. Or the bowling god. They operate under the delusion that a smoother run through the moguls or a higher bowling average will result in greater significance.

Men of wisdom find significance in God. Authentic, lasting significance is rooted in Christ. Jesus said, "I am the vine; you are the branches. If a man remains in me and I in him, he will bear much fruit; apart from me you can do nothing" (John 15:5). That is to say, a man cannot find significance apart from Christ. Only when he submits everything to God's agenda can he satisfy his greatest need in a way that endures.

Karl Haffner is an author and pastor in Washington state.

During televised interviews, NBC and CBS called him a hero. The National Enquirer *splashed his picture before their entire reading audience. Through all the publicity, it is the absolute conviction of this author that a man's love of and commitment to God is most thoroughly expressed when he puts another's life and needs before his own.*

The Unlikeliest Hero

by Robert Wilson

Dr. Gawin Flynn lay before me, pulseless and nonbreathing. In the background, I could hear the shrieking sirens of the police and the fire and rescue squad as they raced down Roderick Road. His wife, Edwina, knelt by his head. The cries of his two sons rang in my ears, "He's dead. Dad's dead!"

It didn't seem possible now, amid all of the panic and confusion, that less than an hour ago, Dr. Flynn's family and mine had been splashing in our pool together, cooling off from the oppressive July heat. Afterward, we munched on a succulent watermelon and sat around discussing the good times and the new hope he had in his recent marriage. We enjoyed each other's company.

I went upstairs to my room to change clothes as everybody else was getting out of the pool. I had just put on my shoes when I heard crying and shrieks. "Help! He's drowning! He's drowning! Oh, God! Dr. Wilson, help us please!"

I went downstairs, through the dining room, grabbed the door, wrenched it open, and ran through the screen, over the deck, and down the steps toward the pool.

I plunged into the deep end, shoes and all, about eight and one-half feet. I sank to the bottom, and there at the side of the pool, my fingers found the body, right where the bottom angled into the sides. He was almost stiff.

I picked him up and dragged him slowly up the side of the pool, but I couldn't get him out. The footing was too slippery. Asking for divine strength, I went underneath him and pushed while his son pulled on one arm and my daughter Valerie pulled on the other. His body shot out of the pool and hit the concrete deck. Immediately, I stretched him out and straightened his head. I felt for the lower back end, and then with the other hand, I pushed under the lungs, expelling the water that was in him. With fluid gushing out, I searched for a pulse. To my horror, there was none.

I massaged his back and quickly struck him with my fist two or three times, then proceeded to push on the diaphragm and seek to establish a breathing pattern again. The concrete was biting into my knees, but I kept working on him, using the techniques I had learned in college, the naval air force, and in Boy Scouts. And, indeed, in later thinking about what I did, it was a curious combination. With the shrieking and wailing of the sirens in the background, I couldn't help but think, *My God, what more can I do? Help me, Lord. Help me.*

Somehow the thought flicked through my mind that it had only been a year ago that I had helped officiate at the wedding of this couple. It had been a wedding of fun, happiness, and hope for the future.

That future now seemed quite uncertain. I couldn't understand how this could have happened.

I was told later that Gawin had gone back into the pool to swim a couple more laps with his boys. Not a strong swimmer, but most certainly a willing father, he swam back and forth, only to find that he was tiring. His strength gave out while standing at the slope of the pool going into the deep end. Edwina held out a pole for him to hold on to while she tried to pull him into the shallow water. But he slowly slid in and under.

Suddenly, I felt a pulsing as my thumb pressed against his artery. Meanwhile, the rescue squad came running down the hill to the edge of the pool. Then he took his first breath. Edwina grabbed me and kissed my cheek.

But the danger was not over yet. He had been under water three to four minutes. Could there be brain damage?

As the rescue squad took over, the police questioned me. I proceeded to tell them, pointing out where the body had been, down at the bottom of the pool. They couldn't understand my actions, my pointing, I guess. I pointed in the general direction of the bottom of the pool.

Finally, Gawin was stabilized and moved to the Frederick Memorial Hospital.

We dressed, and my daughter drove us to the emergency room. News must have spread fast, because the receptionist kept calling me a hero. She proceeded to take us back to the treatment room, enunciating some of the virtues I had never thought of myself as having.

The Unlikeliest Hero

Edwina came quickly to me, hugging me and repeating, "He's alive! He's alive." I thought then that it was time for a prayer and thanksgiving. Going to the bed where Gawin shivered under the sheets, still in wet swim trunks, I grasped his hand and felt the firmness and the strength in it again.

A few minutes later, the police chief came and shook my hand. "Dr. Wilson, you're a hero." I kind of smiled at this categorization and asked what he would do if his friend were in a similar predicament. He promptly answered that he'd try to do the same. "Nevertheless," he said, "you're unique, very unique. You can do anything you set your mind to do."

In the humor of the moment, I asked him if he would sign his name, in that he trusted me so much, to a driver's certificate. Of course, he refused that. He felt that I should be able to see if I was to drive! Oh, well. You can't win them all.

Around 1:00 p.m. that night, after trying unsuccessfully to sleep, I put on my wet bathing suit and hit the pool. Diving into the deep end, I found the debris, poles, and all sorts of junk that was used to try to keep Gawin afloat. Again I sensed the struggle that this good woman and her two children had put up to try to save their husband and father. Coming to that same spot at the end of the pool where the body lay inert, only five hours before, I knelt and thanked God for His guidance.

Even though he lost his sight in 1950 while in the naval air force, Robert Wilson has saved the lives of three people—two from drowning, and believe it or

49

not, he caught one man when he fell off a high ladder. After being discharged, Wilson went to college to receive his BA, his master's, and then his doctorate in sociology. He taught at Columbia Union College for twenty-one years. He is now on the board of directors of Christian Record Services and *Amazing Facts*. He also serves on the Human Relations Committee of the North American Division of Seventh-day Adventists.

*"Blessed is the man who does this, the man who holds it fast,
who keeps the Sabbath without desecrating it."
Isaiah 56:2, NIV.*

Miracle at Sea

by Norman Moe

He was a weather-beaten giant who smelled like he'd just taken a bath in beer. His six-and-a-half-foot, 270-pound hulk towered above me as I sat in the pilot's cabin of my boat *Prince*.

"I need a job," he announced rather abruptly. "Name's Egor. Heard you were heading out for a catch tomorrow."

"Well, yes." I stroked my chin, trying to figure out how to politely turn him down. But since he didn't waste any words, I decided that tactfulness wouldn't make any difference with this man.

"I am leaving tomorrow, but I don't think you'll be happy working for me. I don't permit any alcohol on this ship, and I drift every Saturday."

He raised his bushy eyebrows in question.

"I keep the Sabbath. Spend all day resting and reading my Bible. You'd be bored."

He shook his head as he turned to leave. "I'll be here at sunup."

That's how I met Egor. He turned out to be a great deckhand, and the week went well, with us catching about eighty fish every day. Then Friday came, and about an hour before sunset, I hauled in all the fishing gear and scrubbed the ship clean.

Egor didn't say anything, but the next morning, I felt the boat shake as he kicked the rigging. "What time is it?" he roared.

I looked up from my Bible to the clock. "Eight-thirty," I yelled back. Half an hour later, he kicked the rigging again. "What time is it?"

I found a cold 7UP and took it to him. He drank a few swigs and tossed the can into the water. "Not the same," he shouted. "Wish I had a beer."

To calm him down, I said, "Relax, Egor. Tomorrow we get 200 fish."

"How do you know that?" he demanded.

"God always blesses me for honoring the Sabbath and gives a double portion on Sunday," I answered. Then the enormity of what I had said hit me. I went into the cabin and prayed, "Lord, forgive me for the presumption, but we do need a double order of fish tomorrow so this man can see that You answer prayer."

The following day we got 275 fish.

I'll never understand why God chose to let me, a plain, ordinary fisherman, be a testimony to so many people. I knew most of the men in the fishing fleet. They considered my boat a highliner because I usually unloaded more fish than the others. One friend of mine approached me in port and said he'd like to punch me out.

I was surprised by his outburst and inquired why. I'll never forget his answer. "Because we work seven days and you lie in your bunk a whole day, and we still can't catch up to you."

After I became a Christian, I vowed that I would only catch what the Bible terms clean fish and that I would always remember God's Sabbath. He's never failed to bless me. I discovered that if we're faithful to God, He's more than faithful to us.

———————————

Norman Moe is a retired commercial fisherman living in Aberdeen, Washington.

*Time and time again the current, like a powerful magnet,
sucked me under and then spewed me out,
hissing and seething like an angry snake.*

———

Swept Into the
River of No Return

by Dan McGee

It was called "the river of no return," and as I stood in the
dawn of the early morning, peering over the edge of a
jagged rock, I could understand why. Ruby Falls was a
massive, class-ten rapid, with flood-stage water that had
developed a roaring hole fifteen to twenty feet deep. Large
white waves and curls rose twenty feet or more into the air.

My father-in-law, Ommer Drury, a retired medical doc-
tor, stood beside me, pointing to where we should run our
rafts to avoid flipping. He had rafted the Idaho rivers for
thirty-five years and was pretty well known as one of the
best river outfitting guides around.

Our group of fifty-five had spent the last two days lei-
surely floating down the calmer part of the Salmon River,
stopping and starting at will, taking time for worship and
fellowship, and sharing stories around the campfire. We
were varied in backgrounds, with four physicians, two

dentists, five schoolteachers, and quite a few teens and retired folk. But today would be more challenging, and Doc drove us downstream to make sure we knew our course.

"Now the next rapid is Lake Creek," I heard him say. "It's a rough monster. Run your raft to the right."

We all nodded and headed back to help break camp. Then we gathered on the beach and listened as Doc gave last-minute instructions and made sure everyone had a life jacket on. I had helped drive the vehicles to the takeout area, so by the time I reached for mine, all the adult life jackets were gone. This would be a real problem for me later in the day.

But for now, the morning sun seemed gentle as fingers of light slowly crept over the mountains. We cast off with excitement mounting. Each bend of the river brought larger rapids as the river picked up more water from mountain streams.

At noon, we stopped at a campsite for lunch and rest. I leaned back and surveyed the whole scene. My wife, smiling and relaxed; my son, electrified over the morning's events and anticipating the rougher water ahead. It was one of those rare moments in time when the worries of the world seem so far away and the sun enfolds you like a warm blanket. So warm, in fact, that I shed my wet suit.

By the time we approached Ruby Rapids, I had a real feel for maneuvering the craft. I ran it just as Doc had told me to. It shot up twenty feet like a roller coaster and drove down into a large whirlpool. I skirted the rapid but still felt its power from the side as I passed.

Then, ahead of us, I spotted Lake Creek Rapids, its white

tip resembling a pot of boiling water. Mine would be the last boat through.

Doc took the rapid head-on, with my son Pat riding out on the front tube. The raft bucked up fifteen feet in the air and came down into a canyon of raging water. Doc's raft had twenty-five passengers on board. His boat weighed two tons loaded, so he easily withstood the volume and waves that went over it.

I had only my wife, Joy, with me, so my raft was very light, especially on the nose. It seemed against my better judgment to follow the same course. By the time we were within a hundred feet of the rapid, I wished that I had followed my instincts.

We were being sucked right into the large canyon! I yelled at Joy to brace herself and to hang on. The next few seconds were unbelievable as a violent wave stopped us in our tracks. The next thing I knew, I was being twisted up in the air and tossed into the river. The oars swung out of my hands. I took a deep breath as my body plunged, headfirst, into the icy depths.

My body immediately went into shock. At five feet under, I looked up and could see the raft right over the top of me. It had righted itself, and somehow I knew that Joy was still in it. I tried to swim up to it but couldn't get out from underneath it. The pain receded into hypothermic euphoria. *I'm drowning*, I thought. *I'm drowning.*

Instinctively, I prayed for the Lord to save me and immediately felt His warm love. His presence calmed me enough to start swimming. I surfaced about ten feet in front of the raft.

Joy was shouting at me to grab the oar, but by then, the turbulent water was tossing me like a rag doll, just out of reach. I briefly saw the shocked faces of those in the other rafts. I heard Doc shouting and pointing for me to swim toward shore, but my body had gone into hypothermia, and I was zapped of all strength. Time and time again, the current, like a powerful magnet, sucked me under and then spewed me out, hissing and seething like an angry snake.

And then it felt as if I had been dumped in calmer waters. My mind told me to swim, but my muscles wouldn't obey. I probably would have sunk to the bottom had not strong arms encircled me and pulled me out. I later learned that my mother-in-law was driving down the forest service road as a safety precaution should an emergency develop. She saw my problem and radioed for help.

So now I sit, pondering the fragile preciousness of life, treasuring the moments I have with my wife and children. I have no doubt that God is real. He spared my life that day. I have been able to preach to my congregation about God's promises with a little more feeling and zest than ever before.

"He is my refuge and my fortress: my God; in him will I trust" (Psalm 91:2, KJV).

Dan McGee wrote this while pastoring in Hoquiam, Washington.

His parachute had collapsed, and there was not enough time
for the rip cord to open the reserve chute. It seemed that
certain death was imminent unless God intervened.

———

The Jump

by Marvin Mosher

The roar from the engines of the C-130 air force plane
obliterated everything but my thoughts. We were on our
way to a drop zone in Germany sometime in the summer of
1960. This would become the one jump with the Eighth Division Airborne paratroopers that I would always remember.

At the age of twenty, I found that God was not a dominant part of my life, but I still said my prayers each night—
and especially before a jump. It was a carry-over from my
early training.

The butterflies exploded in my stomach as the five-
minute warning light flashed on beside the open door of
the plane. The jump master signaled for us to stand and
hook up our static lines to the overhead cable, which
would deploy our chutes as we jumped away from the
plane.

During the next five minutes, each man checked his own

equipment and the man's in front of him. I said another prayer.

The red light flashed green, and all thoughts were drowned out as the line of men started forward, shouting, "Go! Go! Go!" The roar of the engines and a two-hundred-mile-per-hour blast of wind greeted me. My chute opened with a hard jerk. Suddenly, it was absolutely still as the feeling of weightlessness took over. No one spoke, as this was a simulated combat jump.

I tried to look up to check my chute. I knew it was open, but I could not raise my head to look up. Maybe I hadn't had my elbow tucked tight to my side when I jumped, for the prop blast had spun me like a top, and my suspension lines were wound up from my chute to the back of my neck. I suddenly knew I was in trouble.

I yelled for the paratrooper directly below me to spill some air from his chute and move out from under me, since I could not control my chute until my suspension lines unwound.

He didn't cooperate. Instead, he froze. His chute created a vacuum, and my chute collapsed. I landed on top of his chute and slid over the side of it into space.

I had jumped from 1,260-feet elevation. That meant that without a chute I would have hit the ground in eight seconds. By the time I came off the other man's chute, I was so low that my reserve chute would not have time to deploy. It seemed my life was about to end. I was going to hit the ground and break every bone in my body. My heart screamed "Jesus!"

As I slid over the edge, I suddenly felt myself being

sucked under his chute. I went back through his suspension lines and became tangled in them. We came down together under his chute.

The normal rate of descent is eighteen to twenty-four feet per second with only one man to a chute. We hit the ground hard—but I was alive and had no injuries except bruises.

Over the years, I have had many close calls with death. God has saved my life over and over again. "For he shall give his angels charge over thee, to keep thee in all thy ways" (Psalm 91:11, KJV). As I look back, I know it was an angel who pushed me sideways into the other chute and saved me. God knew that should I be spared, I would eventually dedicate my whole life to Him. He could see beyond the years, to the co-workers and family whom I would influence to follow Him.

Life takes many paths as the Lord gently leads us toward an encounter with Him. I am thankful for that leading. It took fourteen years of His nudging before I knelt in humble surrender at the cross.

Since then, He has led me to train as a lay pastor, Revelation Seminar leader, and elder in the church. Others have been led to the watery grave of baptism because of His leading in my life. My one goal is to be ready when Jesus comes for me and to have as many others ready as possible.

Marvin Mosher operates a roofing and construction business in Rockwell, North Carolina.

His parents were cruelly murdered when he was only five years old. He spent most of his early years hiding in the mountain jungle, surviving with relatives who did not welcome his presence. Would he ever be able to forgive?

Bent on Revenge

by Hector Gayares

Bits and pieces of that night will always remain vivid in my mind. The machine guns blasting the stillness of the evening. Screams of agony. Men yelling something that I couldn't understand. My older brother grabbing my hand and urging me to run, run, run and not look back. I became an orphan that night at five-and-a-half years old.

Life had been fairly peaceful until World War II came to our area of the Philippines in 1941. The Japanese Imperial Army gained control of the entire country when the Allied Forces in Corregidor surrendered on May 6, 1942.

But some of the Filipino soldiers did not surrender. They went to the hills and mountains to start guerilla resistance. These small bands of guerilla fighters would ambush Japanese soldiers who patrolled the towns and villages. When the resistance fighters killed Japanese soldiers, the Japanese retaliated by preying on the helpless civilians in the villages, killing men, women, and children by the use of bayonets.

Eventually, the Japanese soldiers occupied our town. Some of the people began to evacuate by hiding in the villages. One late afternoon, as darkness began to settle, some guerilla fighters ambushed and killed Japanese soldiers not far from the village where my family hid. Since the ambush happened toward evening, most of the people in the neighboring villages were unaware of their potential peril. All seemed peaceful that night.

But at dawn while everyone slept, the crack of gunfire shattered the stillness. As people fled from their homes, they were mowed down unmercifully. Women screamed, children cried, men shouted, and dogs barked. The peaceful village had been transformed into hell.

Many ran for their lives and hid in thick bushes and nipa swamps. My elder brother grabbed my six-month-old-sister, and together we jumped from the bamboo hut and ran. My aunt and uncle kept shouting for me to run faster and not look back. I ran as fast as I could, and yet they kept shouting for me to run faster. I shall always remember the terror I felt as each step took me away from my mother.

Unfortunately for both of them, my father was sick. He tried to flee with my mother supporting him. But they could not run fast. They were overcome by Japanese soldiers and cruelly bayoneted to death.

Later in the day, some of the braver people came out from their hiding places. Upon learning that the soldiers had left to regroup, they began looking for missing family members and friends. They found my poor father with no less than twenty bayonet wounds all over his body. My mother's skull was blown away from her head by a bullet through the right eye. That was January 15, 1943.

My parents were hurriedly buried near the spot where they fell. Everyone feared that the Japanese might return. There was not a moment to lose. Most of the people who survived, including my uncles and aunts, decided to evacuate to the mountains.

Life became more difficult for all of us, as food was scarce, and there was no adequate shelter or clothing. Miraculously, my six-month-old sister and I survived. But the death of my parents affected me so much. I cried bitterly, wondering how we could exist without my father and mother. Why were both of them taken so cruelly while we were so small? What was to become of us? The questions tumbled about in my young mind. I cried because there was no answer.

So I grew up in a hostile environment. The three of us lived with my uncle, whose wife treated us terribly, especially my little sister. My aunt didn't want the burden of young children. Now, I can understand that she, too, carried a heavy load, but all I knew then was that we were unloved and unwanted. Even my teachers seemed unkind. I developed a hatred toward the Japanese, my aunt, my teacher, and everyone else who I thought was bad to me. Revengeful feelings dominated my life.

I did not know about love. I could not experience my mother's adoration, her kiss, or her hug. I could not remember my mother's prayers or feel her concern. I did not know that there was a loving Saviour who felt the pain and read the heart. All I knew was scolding, cursing, and angry words directed at us from morning until night.

And like a cancer, hate began to eat me inch by inch. Anger, bitterness, and revenge gnawed at my soul.

I'm so grateful God had a plan for me—that He sent to our town an evangelist, who stood in the plaza and preached the gospel of Jesus Christ. He told me of a loving God, a loving Father, and a loving Saviour. I was drawn to Jesus Christ and the truth. Assured of His love and forgiveness, I poured out all my heart to Jesus, and for the first time, I found peace and forgiveness for those who had mistreated me.

I began to work for their salvation. My uncle decided to accept Jesus as his personal Saviour, and when I was ordained to the gospel ministry, I had the privilege of baptizing him.

In 1991, when Japan celebrated the fiftieth anniversary of the Japanese declaration of war in the Pacific, I was invited to hold "Peace and Friendship Revival Crusades" in Japan. Only God made it possible for me to stand in front of the Japanese people, who were responsible for the death of my parents, and tell them of Jesus Christ. I can honestly say that I love them and that I forgave them because the love of Jesus made it so.

Hector Gayares is the president of the Central Philippine Union Mission in Cebu City.

Section 3

Overcoming Our Adversary

Be strong in the Lord,
and in the power of his might.
Put on the whole armor of God,
that ye may be able to stand against the
wiles of the devil.
For we wrestle not against flesh and
blood, but against principalities,
against powers, against the rulers
of darkness of this world,
against spiritual wickedness in high
places.

———————

Ephesians 6:10-12, KJV.

*A biologist outwits a hungry hawk
and in the process
learns one of life's most valuable lessons.*

———

Snares of the Fowler

by Richard D. Brown, Ph.D.

It flapped a few strong beats, then literally disappeared. I was looking through binoculars and had glanced away for just a split second. Had the bird discovered my hiding place? Systematically, I searched the blue sky back and forth. It was nowhere in sight!

I am a biologist. Ever since I can remember, I have enjoyed the study of God's creatures. My earliest memories include climbing trees to get a bird's-eye view, collecting insects, spending nights at the local farm pond with flashlight in hand catching noisy frogs and toads, and grabbing garter snakes with grubby hands, trying not to get bitten. Didn't matter much if I did. I quickly learned that the bite didn't hurt as much as people said it would. What did hurt, I later discovered, were the "bites" of people!

My dad worked as an industrial emergency nurse. Although I am now fifty-three, I can vividly remember the time he brought home a beautiful polyphemus moth that had been lured to the bright lights at the plant and died from exhaustion. Dad and Mom encouraged me to enjoy the out-of-doors and to glean from nature the many lessons God had placed there.

Now, as a sort of professional hobby, I band birds, especially hawks. I am like the fowler mentioned in Psalm 91:3: "Surely he shall deliver thee from the snare of the fowler."* I put out several types of traps and use live lures to attract birds of prey. Unlike the devil, I do them no harm. Each is identified, aged, sexed, measured, and then given a U.S. Fish and Wildlife Service band. A great amount of knowledge about bird behavior has been learned through trapping and banding.

I sit concealed in a blind looking through small holes. When I spot a hawk, I pull ropes to make the lures move. Then the hungry hawk and I do battle. "They are passed away as the . . . eagle that hasteth to the prey" (Job 9:26). The hawk hasn't the slightest idea what I am up to. It is alert, strong, and instinctively cunning. But so am I.

Here it comes! I get goose bumps as my eye catches the hawk coming in on an incredibly steep and swift glide, with folded wings and feet ready. The hawk has seen my lure from about a mile out. With folded wings, the hawk becomes a tiny projectile that my eyes can no longer see. The lure has worked! I've snared the hawk.

Over the years, I have caught thousands of birds and hundreds of hawks. I have had to sit and wait patiently. There has been plenty of time to watch . . . and think. The lessons are many, and some are hard. While I don't like to admit it, when banding, I play the role of that old serpent, the devil.

I use only a few kinds of snares: mist nets, bow traps, Balchatries, Verbails, and Dho-gazas. But Satan uses numerous snares. He is so good that he makes very specific traps for just you and just me. We are talking predator-prey battle here.

What snares are likely to catch you? Delicious food? Strong drink? Something that excites the nervous system? Attractive, exciting shows on TV? Pretty women? Lustful magazines? The deacon's new car? A friendly relationship gone too far? The strong need for friends—so you listen and laugh at that shady joke?

As a fowler myself, I urge you to be on constant guard. I want you to know that the devil is not going to use a snare that will not work. I spend hours perfecting my traps. So why shouldn't he? I am talking frankly here. This is battle. The snares are real. The lures are extremely attractive. The game is not fair. For you and me, it can be deadly. We need to pray for strength to be delivered "as a roe from the hand of the hunter, and as a bird from the hand of the fowler" (Proverbs 6:5).

What wonderful lessons God intends for us to learn through His creation, no matter what our age. I am concerned that many of us ignore His second book. Spend time outside learning from Him. Encourage your children or grandchildren to learn of God through His creation. Do whatever it takes.

The Lord has likened Himself to the largest of hawks, the

POWER FOR EVERYDAY HEROES

mighty eagle. "As an eagle stirreth up her nest, fluttereth over her young, spreadeth abroad her wings, taketh them, beareth them on her wings: so the Lord alone did lead him [Jacob], and there was no strange god with him" (Deuteronomy 32:11, 12). God cares for us as an eagle cares for her young.

An eagle always surrounds God's throne. "And the first beast was like a lion, and the second beast like a calf, and the third beast had a face as a man, and the fourth beast was like a flying eagle" (Revelation 4:7). He likens His church to an eagle. "To the woman were given two wings of a great eagle, that she might fly into the wilderness, into her place, where she is nourished for a time, and times, and half a time, from the face of the serpent" (Revelation 12:14). God has high hopes for us. He wants us to fly away from the temptations of the devil and to dwell with Him forever in the wilderness of peace.

"Watch and pray, that ye enter not into temptation: the spirit indeed is willing, but the flesh is weak" (Matthew 26:41). "Watch ye therefore, and pray always, that ye may be accounted worthy to escape all these things that shall come to pass, and to stand before the Son of man" (Luke 21:36).

Be an eagle. Fly strong. Fly high. But be constantly on the watch for the snares of the fowler.

*All Bible Verses taken from the King James Version.

Richard Brown is a biology professor and environmental consultant living in Supply, North Carolina.

He founded the Carolina Raptor Center. His favorite hobbies are hawk watching and hawk banding.

*He didn't want to pull the trigger. There would be no
second chance if he missed or wounded the bear.
But what does one do when there is only eight feet between
you and certain death?*

The Intruder

by Ron Rogers

As I looked through the scope on my Mini 14 rifle, I
could barely discern the outline of his head. Just a blurry
shape at eight feet away. I couldn't take aim any other way
except through the scope. Questions raced through my
mind. What if I missed? What would he do? If I should miss,
how much damage would be done to my car, sitting fifty
feet directly behind the blur in my scope? What if I just
wounded him? The screen door was the only tangible thing
between us. He could knock it down as easily as I could
knock over a matchbox! And what if I didn't shoot him? He
didn't look as if he were planning on leaving anytime soon.
How many times had I chased him away? And yet here he
was at three o'clock in the morning, more brazen and more
aggressive than before.

The bear had come to our back porch shortly after sun-
down. I chased him away. About 10:30, just as I was pre-

paring for bed, I heard a noise. I opened the back door and saw wet footprints. I got my flashlight and went to the woodshed to get a few more pieces of wood for the stove, and there he was, not more than fifteen feet away! I shined the light in his eyes and yelled at him. He ran slowly to the other end of the house. I followed him with my trusty flashlight and yelled at him again. This time, he stopped and growled at me. I flickered the light in his eyes really fast, and he finally went off into the woods. I thought that should be the end of him for the night.

Approximately 2:00 a.m., I suddenly awoke. I felt a sense of uneasiness and could not go back to sleep. After tossing and turning for a while, I decided to get up and read. I had been reading for about ten minutes when I heard a scratching sound on the back porch.

I turned on the porch light and opened the door. Wet bear prints again! I reasoned that if I left the door open and the porch light on, certainly he wouldn't return again. A few minutes later, he was back on the porch. I thought, *This is a crazy, crazy bear.*

I reached up, turned off the lamp, grabbed my gun, then tiptoed to within a few feet of the door. Surely he would smell me and run away. But no! He came right to the screen door and began to push his nose against it. I thought, *This bear is not just prowling. He's not just crazy. This bear is dangerous!*

My wife, Cheryl, slept peacefully in the bedroom, totally unaware of the immediate danger she was in. What if he were to catch her out in the yard alone? What would happen? What could happen?

POWER FOR EVERYDAY HEROES

With the thoughts of what could happen, my decision was made. With the rifle carefully poised, I peeked around the side of the scope so I could see the bear clearly. There he was, his wet nose against the nylon screen, pushing it in. Only eight feet between me and a beast so large he could crush me to death with one blow. His hair glistened in the porch light. The vapor from his breath in the cold air rolled through the screen door into the kitchen. As he breathed, he made some intimidating grunting noises. He seemed to be using his sense of smell to the max, sniffing and snorting. His mouth appeared to be drooling. His massive shoulders filled the outline of the doorway.

He grunted loudly and brought my mind back to the last question. What if Cheryl met him alone? The possibilities brought forth a sense of anger at his intrusion.

I looked back through the scope, and all I could see was this black blur. I couldn't define his chest through the scope. I needed a heart or head shot. There would be no second chance. Searching through the scope, I could see the blurry outline of what appeared to be his head. No features of his face were discernable through the scope. The cross hairs would not be accurate at eight feet.

My heart pumped, and I could feel the adrenalin rushing through my body as my finger began to slowly squeeze the trigger. Tighter and tighter, until suddenly—BANG! The sound of the rifle was deafening in the quiet of the night.

The huge bear rose off his front feet into a sitting position, then rolled right over backward, down the steps to the ground. I rushed out, ready to shoot again, but there was no need. The bear never moved after he landed at the bottom of the steps.

Talk about a rude awakening for my wife! She grabbed her robe and rushed out the door to see the maverick who had been vandalizing our home and several other homes in the general neighborhood.

She stood there for a few moments, silently looking at the bear, then asked, "Are you sure he's dead?"

"Yes," I answered. "You don't need to worry. You won't meet up with him in the woods."

I looked for the location of the entrance and possible exit of the bullet and noticed that a notch had been cut in his right ear. That notch indicated that he had been a problem bear somewhere else and had been relocated to our area.

Now, understand, I am not a hunter. I don't hunt bears, but because of where I live (so far back in the woods that it's four miles to my mailbox), wisdom tells me to be prepared in case I am confronted. Therefore, since I am no match physically for a bear, I possess something that can overcome a bear.

I often think of that "ole" bear. Why did he do the things he did? What made him lose his fear of man? I have drawn some spiritual correlations in my own mind that I'd like to share with you.

I have likened the old bear to the devil. The devil has no consideration or respect for my home or life. Neither did the bear. Like the bear, the devil comes with cunning; then at times he brazenly pushes himself into our lives and disrupts the harmony we enjoy with God and our fellow man. Like the bear, he causes anxiety and fear. He harasses and vandalizes our lives and would most certainly take our life physically and, even more so, spiritually, if allowed to.

As I contended with that bear, I certainly was no match for him in physical strength, for standing toe to toe and hand to hand, he could have torn me apart. The same is true with the devil. We are no match for him in our strength. Fighting with him alone would be suicide. As a matter of fact, we should never get involved in fighting with him at all. As our adversary, he is already defeated. Our Elder Brother has already contended with him hand to hand and toe to toe, if you please, and has defeated him. Jesus is His name, and His victory is our victory.

Ron Rogers is a physical therapist who sold his business in a city and moved to the wooded mountains of Virginia. There, Ron and Cheryl built a home with some unique back-to-basics features. Instead of an electric refrigerator, Ron constructed a long wooden box and piped a continuous flow of cold creek water through it. They report that it works wonderfully for everything except frozen products.

Section 4

Tools of Our Trade

Seest thou a man diligent in his business? he shall stand before kings.

———————————

Proverbs 22:29, KJV.

Not being open on Saturdays in a highly competitive business can be devastating. One businessman explains his secret to success.

Faithful in All Things— Even Business

by Donn Leiske

There are some decided competitive disadvantages to being a Seventh-day Adventist business owner. An Adventist contractor, for instance, may miss out on some high-paying contracts because he is not open on Friday evenings or Saturdays. He also gives tithes and offerings and supports Christian education. With these and other apparent business limitations, why, then, are Seventh-day Adventist business owners as successful, if not more so, than those who are not Christians?

A great number of Adventist men are self-employed. Maybe because of conflict of interest with labor union strategies. Maybe because of Sabbath work-scheduling difficulties. It might even be that Adventists are independent thinkers, therefore, more likely to be self-employed. Whatever the reason, it appears that the percentage of self-employed men is higher among Seventh-day Adventists than among the general population.

We who become self-employed, or own a business, rarely have intensive training in business, despite the fact that Adventist men seem to have a higher level of education than the overall male population. The business department is not typically one of the strongest departments at our educational institutions. After all, we believe we're on this earth to be missionaries to a lost world and not just to perfect the skills of accumulating personal wealth. So, even if we are well educated, we probably enter business unprepared.

How is it, then, that we succeed in such a competitive market, with little training and a nonworldly motivation for having a business in the first place?

Successful Seventh-day Adventist businesspeople work hard. But so do non-Adventist businesspeople. We learn on the job and take advantage of training opportunities. But so do others. So what is the secret to success for the Adventist businessperson?

The secret is in Psalm 84:11, "The Lord will give grace and glory: no good thing will he withhold from them that walk uprightly."

A favorite example of mine is an experience that happened to me in our business. SHOPWARE, Inc., produces training and testing software for vocational education. Most of our customers are teachers. We market our products through dealers, catalogs that we send to schools, and exhibitions at appropriate trade shows.

Fortunately, almost all trade shows have few or no Sabbath scheduling conflicts. The main exception is the largest international show in our industry. This is the most expensive show that we attend. Not only does this two-and-a-half-day show include Sabbath, but Sabbath is opening day!

It is our company practice that our monthly administrative meetings always begin with prayer, even if the meeting includes a non-Christian or non-Adventist. We prayed before we first discussed attending this most important show. This resulted in a plan to attend, but not on Sabbath.

We discussed whether to tell the show planners that we would not be there on Sabbath or to keep our plan silent and see what would happen. We decided it would be more honest if we warned them ahead of time. A prime booth location was selected from the floor map, and we mailed our application, with a small note that we would not be staffing our booth on Saturday.

Soon we received communication that all exhibitors must have their booths staffed at all times, and this rule had never been violated. The letter writing soon turned into direct phone conversations, and we explained the biblical reasons for our decision. They asked if we could get permission from some church authority to make an exception this time. We explained that it was our choice and that this was a nonnegotiable item. They had a special board meeting and discussed our situation.

Their response was that in all the years of administering the show, they had never had a request of this kind, even though the largest floor space on the map was purchased by a Jewish company from Israel. We thought this was interesting in that the show also included a full day on Sunday,

81

and there would be many Sunday-keeping Christians as exhibitors.

They agreed to allow us to not staff our booth on Saturday, but we had to give up our prime booth location in exchange for a less visible place, with low traffic flow. We agreed, knowing we would be losing in the process.

Following the example of an Adventist-owned company in another industry, we made a red sign that we placed in the most obvious spot in our booth that said *Free demonstrations tomorrow. "And God rested on the seventh day" (Genesis 2:2, KJV) . . . and we've done the same.*

We enjoyed that first day of the show with the local church congregation . . . all the while eager to see what would be the result of our not attending opening day.

The following Sunday morning I will never forget. Many show participants came by our booth and said, "We missed you on Saturday and made sure to come back to see you today." This was in spite of the fact that this show is so large that many people never see all of the exhibits! One of the exhibitors, who was also one of our dealers, came by our booth to tell us how impressed they were that we were willing to go to such expense to stand up for our beliefs and how much of a good influence we were to people for our commitment. They said that the Saturday traffic had been very low and that we hadn't missed anything! It was exciting to see God work!

The Lord has since blessed us every year as we have stood up for Him. Our ability to witness at this yearly show has resulted in impact on other dealers. One business owner's husband became a committed vegetarian, and the owner has read numerous Adventist books with great interest.

The show administrators no longer discuss our not attending on Sabbath, because they know we won't be there. We are now allowed to pick any booth location that we want on the show floor. And on at least one occasion, we have had a person come up to us and explain that he was raised an Adventist and was backslidden. He appreciated our witness and our way of doing business.

God has made sure that we succeed in business equal to, or better than, a non-Adventist business. But more importantly, we have seen that the best rewards are not measured with a business calculator.

Yes, there are some decided competitive disadvantages in being a Seventh-day Adventist business owner, but there is an even more important advantage. God promises in Matthew 6:33, "Seek ye first the kingdom of God, and his righteousness; and all these things shall be added unto you" (KJV).

Donn Leiske is a husband and father of two. He is the head elder of the Grays Harbor Seventh-day Adventist Church in Aberdeen, Washington. Donn has been a teacher and has been self-employed several times. He and his wife, Kathie, own SHOPWARE, Inc., a computer software business.

From his lofty perch on a twelve-foot ladder,
a hammer in one hand and a nail in the other,
Melvin Brannon contemplates what it's like to be

———

The Carpenter's Son

by Melvin Brannon

Maybe carpentry was a natural tendency, the logical thing for a shy country boy like me to do. After all, I was following in my father's footsteps. Was that so bad? But I struggled with the decision. What about those hot summer days that could boil your brain? Or the way your hands would crack and bleed in the cold of winter? Statistics proved it to be a hazardous occupation. It certainly would not be a glamorous job, and "common laborers" aren't regarded as very high on the social ladder.

I didn't plan to spend my life subjecting my brain and body to that much strain. But in spite of my plans, there were plenty of job offers for someone with my knowledge and skills in carpentry when school ended. I guess that somewhere in the back of my mind, I admired my dad's ability to perform. The job offers kept coming, and as long as there was work. . . .

The Carpenter's Son

As the years passed, I realized that carpentry didn't leave a man much to look forward to. My creative handiwork would probably never receive its due acclaim. I would never be able to drive enough nails to ensure prosperity. I spent a lot of time rubbing liniment on sore, aching muscles. I pampered those multiple pinched nerves and protected those delicate sinus membranes. I also developed a tremendous void as I watched the years go by without accomplishment, without seeing any dreams fulfilled.

As I meditated on my dilemma, I realized that there had never been any abrupt changes in my life, except for a few times when I acted on reflex. The same was true when I became a Christian. I couldn't even recall one "blockbuster" moment in my experience that I could say, "This is when I found the Lord!" My conversion was just a gradual series of events and bits of knowledge that later led to rational decisions concerning biblical truths.

It took me many years to discover that the balance I was looking for in my life was impossible to find because my goal was wrong. I was trying to use my *physical* being to reach that elusive dream.

I found that the Bible uses terminology and analogies that show the world through the eyes of a Master Builder. This earth and everything in it were conceived by infinite wisdom and constructed by creative genius.

Jesus promised, just before He went back to heaven, to prepare mansions for His people. How awesome! The Creator, who walked among men as a carpenter's son, would now build a most spectacular edifice, the Holy City, the New Jerusalem. He even took the time to give us a condensed blueprint of its appearance and a partial list of building materials.

This stuff was right down my alley! Why hadn't I paid attention to these things before? If I desired, I could be one of those "lively stones" in that spiritual house. I could use the talents God has given me to construct things with eternal longevity. If I used Jesus as the Chief Cornerstone, my endeavors would produce something of everlasting quality. Added to the beauty of knowing these things was the privilege of applying construction principles that are written in the universal laws of heaven. What incentive! This was what I needed, what I wanted.

To help others find Jesus and eternal salvation while "on the job" was a dream come true. My priorities had been all mixed up. I had been building too many things on shifting sands and disallowing the Cornerstone, the Rock of Salvation. Now I knew why the Lord had allowed me to grow up on a farm. Hard work and simple values were only the first step in balancing worldly and spiritual goals. To succeed at what you want to accomplish here on earth is only part of true success. To become part of God's kingdom in the process is a bonus worth striving for.

My favorite verses in the Bible held the answer all along. "Come unto me, all ye that labour and are heavy laden, and I will give you rest" (Matthew 11:28, KJV). The next two verses hold the key to the peace I longed for. Jesus talked of being meek and lowly, a necessary attribute. He reminded me to take His yoke, which is easy, and His burden, which is light. A yoke or a burden stands for service in these verses. Whether it refers to physical or spiritual service, the logic seems to fit. He never told me I would be without a burden or yoke, only that they would be easy with Him.

I am a carpenter just like my father. And I am striving to become like my Saviour, who was once a humble carpenter here on this earth but is now the Master Builder. He has accepted me as His son. I hope that the things I have learned here on earth will contribute to the building of projects of cosmic value, not only for myself, but for those who may learn from me.

Melvin Brannon is a carpenter living in Charlotte, North Carolina.

Tim Allen's popular television program Home Improve-ment *has been at the top in ratings for some time now. But what could that possibly have to do with a men's devotional?*

———

Tool Time With Jesus

by Carlton Mosher

What could Tim Taylor, of the popular television pro-gram *Home Improvement,* have in common with Jesus and myself? And maybe you?

The sitcom is about an egotistical male who hosts a low-rated TV show called *Tool Time.* Tim's wife, Jill, can never understand her husband's fascination with power and speed, all of which he creates with tools. Tools are his best friends. With them, he can win a lawn mower race and outwit another competitor for having the most original decorations at Christmas (his reindeer really flies, and of course his lights illuminate the whole neighborhood).

Could it be that we all love tools? The power to create with our own hands? Perhaps that's why I am a carpenter. I do the very best work I can, using the very best tools available to me. Somehow I feel that Jesus did the work of a master carpenter. He had skill and flawless qualities. He never left a job undone or quoted the familiar saying "that's good enough." And no doubt His tools were the best available to Him.

Not long ago, I was asked at the last minute to tell a story for the children at church. I ran out to my truck to search for an object lesson. All I could find was my trusty tool pouch. But I took it inside and took out one tool at a time, showing it to the children.

I illustrated the sharpness of my utility knife on an old piece of carpet. The words that Jesus spoke are still sharper than any two-edged sword. The tape measure that Jesus used will measure us by our characters. His level will let us know whether we are straight up or on the level.

I found something else inspirational in my tool pouch. Three magnetic cabinet door catches. As I took them out of my apron, I noticed how they had attached themselves together in perfect alignment, all pulling together in the same direction, held by an unseen magnetic force. I thought of our heavenly Father's love and grace and how it is directed toward us and is matched only by the willingness of His dear Son Jesus to pay a price with His life for our sin and mistakes. And the Holy Spirit, who guides, comforts, and sustains us. So must our lives be aligned with Christ's life if we are to experience the magnetic attraction of His saving grace and love. You just need to ask, to come as you are. God will measure and sharpen you and make you a new man, fit for His kingdom. All three of the Godhead will pull together in the same loving direction for our salvation.

Jesus said, "I, if I be lifted up from the earth, will draw all men unto me (John 12:32).*

POWER FOR EVERYDAY HEROES

As we use the tools of our trade, whatever they may be, Jesus admonishes us to "let your light so shine before men, that they may see your good works, and glorify your Father which is in heaven" (Matthew 5:16).

* All texts used are taken from the King James Version.

———————

Carlton Mosher is a carpenter living in Kannapolis, North Carolina. He and his wife, Shirley, have three children and five grandchildren.

Section 5

Relationships

*Be kind and compassionate
to one another, forgiving each other,
just as in Christ God forgave you.*

———————

Ephesians 4:32.

*Faithful friends are life's greatest treasures.
But can you trust another male
with the intimate details of your life?*

———

A Good Friend
Is Hard to Find!

by Len McMillan

Two men met in a cafe along the waterfront, embraced robustly (with the required backslapping, of course), conversed briefly about some recent activities, then moved on to this dialogue:

"So how are you *really?*"

"OK—as good as can be expected. You?"

"Same; I know what you mean."

"Yeah."

"Yeah . . ."

"Yeah . . . it's heavy. . . ."

"It is heavy."

"It's not easy. . . ."

"I know what you mean: it never is."

"But, hey, no pain, no gain."

"Pain's good for you."

"That's what they say. . . ."

"So what else is new?"

What did these two men really say? Hopefully, they both knew each other well enough to *hear* the deeper meaning behind their male grunts and monosyllabic phrases. What these two men were really expressing was the pain of male isolation and alienation.

We men seldom allow ourselves an opportunity to get to know other men in ways that permit a mutual exchange of feelings. Men seldom talk about their personal feelings, preferring, instead, to talk about their accomplishments. The sad fact is that most men simply do not trust each other enough to become good friends. Men stare, stalk, and survey each other but seldom reveal intimate details about their life to other men. Someone once compared the introduction of two men to two dogs circling around and sniffing each other.

Studies indicate that men seem to use the word *but* quite frequently in conversation, while women tend to use *and*, which implies that men are naturally more argumentative than women in our culture. *But* is the conversational crossed sword that sends two men into combat. Competition keeps men at a distance. Distance breeds ignorance. Ignorance breeds prejudice. And prejudice is the precursor to violence and war.

When men delve into the unfamiliar territory of bonding and friendship, they often find themselves ill-equipped to establish real friends. Males are schooled in the arena of power, competition, one-upmanship, and winning at all costs. Because of their competitive upbringing, many men have only one friend—their spouse or girlfriend. Males consider it permissible to verbalize their feelings with a woman but may feel uneasy sharing with another man.

Because of the *male mystique*, many men try desperately to feel what they *ought* to feel, desire what they are *supposed* to desire, and like what they *should* like. Manhood is a very neat package, with no loose strings of emotions to get caught in the conveyer belt of life. Unfortunately, this tightly wrapped package precludes most men from ever experiencing the bonding of intimate friendship with another male.

I remember a bonding that occurred between myself and a man almost twenty-five years my senior. I always thought of it as a father-and-son relationship, until one day he said, "Len, I love you." Tears welled up in his eyes as we embraced.

I choked back my tears and mumbled, "I love you too." As we hugged and slapped each other on the back (real men do not hug without pounding each other on the back), he concluded, "My only regret is that someone did not give me permission to say that seventy years ago."

How sad that men have been taught it is not permissible to verbally express love to another man. As we mature and develop our adult personality, we often build up layers of control and repression. We are taught to deny our emotions, or at least to express them in a way that is acceptable to the *male mystique*. Protecting our sense of manhood is often more important to us than developing close personal relationships. Love for another man is demonstrated with a handshake. Love for a child becomes strong discipline or gift giving. Love for a woman becomes sexual domination.

Sadly, many men walk through life encased in a suit of emotional armor lest anyone think them not a man.

History, literature, and the Bible reveal (although rarely) camaraderie and devotion between two men. Huckleberry Finn and Tom Sawyer, Tonto and the Lone Ranger, Butch Cassidy and the Sundance Kid, Captain Kirk and Mr. Spock, as well as David and Jonathan, are all examples of an intimate relationship between two men. Such relationships may become deeper and more endearing than those between male and female: "A friend who sticks closer than a brother" (Proverbs 18:24).

The friendship between David (soon-to-be king of Israel) and Jonathan (son of the current king) illustrates true male bonding and friendship. The obstacles in their relationship were seemingly overwhelming. First, David had been anointed by the prophet Samuel as the next king of Israel, when it should have been Jonathan's position by birthright. Furthermore, Jonathan's father, Saul, hated David and was determined to kill him. In spite of these and other obstacles, the bond between them was so strong that both men continued to risk their lives in order to remain friends (see 1 Samuel 20).

True friends are more than acquaintances. "A friend loves at all times" (Proverbs 17:17). That means through good times and bad. During times of stress as well as joy. During adolescence and midlife. In fact, "Greater love has no one than this, that he lay down his life for his friends" (John 15:13).

The ultimate compliment Jesus could give His disciples was, "I no longer call you servants. . . . Instead, I have called you friends" (John 15:15).

If you want to learn how to establish male friendships, study the life and friendships of Jesus. True friends are forever and can be depended upon during a time of crisis. True friendship will bond even closer during crisis, while acquaintances and golfing buddies quietly slink away.

Faithful friends are life's greatest treasure, and being a true friend is one of the identifying marks of a real man. Jesus commanded men (and women) to "love each other as I have loved you" (John 15:12). Establishing friendships is not an option; it is a biblical command.

Dr. Len McMillan is a family life specialist in the Potomac Conference of Seventh-day Adventists. His books include *Parent Teen* and *First Class Male*.

He was a common laborer, clock puncher, wage earner. He shopped at the local thrift store, and he smiled on a rainy Monday morning when everything was going wrong.

———

The Builder

by David Merrill

It's 5:30 a.m., and my heavy eyes resist the call to awaken. Still tired from the previous day's labor and concerns, I must enter again the workaday world. So often it seems like an endless grind. Few rewards, and after years of committed hard work, little (of a monetary nature) to show for it.

So I roll to an upright position and turn my soul to my Lord. For a moment, I think, *Lord, You know all about this.* Jesus lived thirty years in the mundane. He was never rewarded monetarily for His hard work and superior skills (carpentry carried no status, just stigma). Then I thought how much is involved in a single verse found in Matthew 13 concerning Jesus and His vocation as a carpenter. "They were astonished, and said, Whence hath this man this wisdom, and these mighty works? Is not this the carpenter's son?" (Matthew 13:54, 55).[1]

Well, I think we can get the message. Carpenters aren't

very wise and mighty. A common laborer, clock puncher, wage earner. That's right; there is no worldly beauty that we should desire Him (see Isaiah 53). A root out of dry ground.

These expressions come to my mind:

"The homage which the world gives to position, or wealth, or talent, was foreign to the Son of Man."[2]

"Human nature is ever struggling for expression, ready for contest; but he who learns of Christ is emptied of self, of pride, of love of supremacy, and there is silence in the soul."[3]

Why was Jesus so popular with the common people? He was one of them! He wasn't middle class. Had He lived today, He might have driven an aging Dodge Dart and shopped at the local thrift store. Our dear Lord was born in poverty and remained there throughout His life on earth.

So often, people who are born in poverty and the lower strata of society are embarrassed about their roots, of the broken-down homes, the constant necessity, and the pressure and problems—yes, desperation—that attends poverty. But Jesus felt favored to be a part of struggling humanity. He wasn't, and isn't, ashamed to call us family.

Jesus lived His life where, by far, most of humanity finds itself. Why did the Saviour choose this circumstance to win back the race? Because He didn't want any soul to feel left out. He knew that the abjectness of most of humanity's lot drives hopeless souls to alcohol, drugs, infidelity, and crime. His purpose was to bring dignity to the bottom of society, to show that real worth and value are actually developed more effectively in these conditions.

POWER FOR EVERYDAY HEROES

Jesus worked with His hands—this is where His wisdom came from; wisdom better known as common sense. Craftsmen deal in the world of physics, with laws that are unforgiving. I know—the greater part of my working life has been spent in practical labor. If you don't calculate right, it just won't work. Jesus learned from this lessons on how to deal with the different elements of the society that surrounded Him in Nazareth, a city known for its perversity and degradation. He was a lily, a bright spot, and an uplifting power that transformed the very fabric of society.

This is our God: quietly bearing burdens, working to provide for us, laboring in obscurity, improving whatever He touches. Jesus wasn't distracted with vanity. He was too focused on building—building tables, doors, cabinets. Building. Building hope and vision in others' lives. Building a perfect character to share with all His brethren—His folks, we His people.

Oh, how quietly God works amidst the millions inhabiting this earth. There is so much sorrow, so much pain. But in it all, there is an immune system at work—a restoring power seeking to heal and transform all to the beautiful character that the man Christ Jesus forged for us in a humble earthly role.

Jesus proved that man's extremity is God's opportunity, that God hasn't left us alone. Even now, He is seeking to wipe our tears from our eyes and make our lives "possible." Can't you picture Christ on a rainy Monday morning when everything is going wrong, when the work is going hard? There He is, lightening the load with His sympathetic presence and indomitable courage.

"He shall not fail nor be discouraged, till he have set judgment in the earth" (Isaiah 42:4).

"A bruised reed shall he not break, and the smoking flax shall he not quench" (verse 3).

I've never been to a third-world country other than northern Mexico. From what I experienced there, and from what I've beheld in magazines and the media, it's plain that the world is filled with bruised reeds and smoking flax. This is evidenced in our lives as well, but God is right with us, wherever we are, high or low, seeking to bring hope and cure to our shameful lives of sin. Seeking to cover us and protect us from embarrassment and confusion—to heal us from the results of our wandering from His great heart of love.

Jesus understands sweat and dust and exhaustion. Protracted problems attended Him continually. Being a good carpenter, He must have been physically developed. Rather than being rough or crude, which usually attends these occupations, He was stable, strong, and sweet. There was majesty in His meekness. It's understandable that John the beloved used that breast to repose on.

> The tools of the trade
> on the Saviour were laid
> The road He must walk
> awfully crude
> But His hands that formed wood
> only knew good
> And brought us salvation from shame.

Jesus the silent, suffering hero, the arm of the Lord—a "Man" for men.

While His life is studied, His sayings are debated and analyzed in the theological seminaries, and His cross is gilded and hung in lush cathedrals, His heart is still with the rough-and-tumble school of hard knocks. By the sweat of His brow, He forged a new trail for you and me. And He is still plugging and struggling for us here today.

When I was a boy, being commanded to mow the lawn or do some other thankless chore usually inspired resistance. But if Dad said, "Let's go out and pick up the yard," somehow that changed the whole thing. So Jesus has honored us with His presence in the occupations of our daily lives, bringing new meaning—yes, fun—to what so often seems brown or gray. What a message to be brought to all whose daily burdens are heavy and hopeless!

1. All Bible texts are taken from the King James Version.
2. *The Desire of Ages*, 260.
3. *Thoughts From the Mount of Blessing*, 15.

David Merrill is a layperson living in Cornville, Arizona. His primary occupation has been general contracting and its attending trades.

The ancient world was a man's world, and women were little more than personal property. How does that fit in with the apostle Paul's counsel to the church?

———

Men for These Times

by Willie Oliver

August 26, July 6, and April 28 are very important dates to me. One August 26 I became a husband. One July 6 I became a father and loved it so much that on April 28, almost three years later, I repeated the joy. My responsibilities in this life are many. However, nothing is more important to me than being Elaine's husband and Jessica and Julian's father.

Analyzing my own life and experience, I have come to the realization that no single element has contributed as greatly to my approach to manhood, husbandhood, and fatherhood as the prayerful, powerful, and positive example of my own father. A man who to me epitomized the best of all three of these dimensions. Dad was strength and kindness, sternness and jocularity, all wrapped up in one.

The apostle Paul speaks most poignantly to the issues of husbandhood and fatherhood, which leads me to believe these matters have been of great importance for a long time.

He wrote: "Husbands, love your wives, just as Christ loved the church and gave himself up for her. . . . In this same way, husbands ought to love their wives as their own bodies. He who loves his wife loves himself. . . . For this reason a man will leave his father and mother and be united to his wife, and the two will become one flesh." "Fathers, do not exasperate your children; instead, bring them up in the training and instruction of the Lord" (Ephesians 5:25, 28, 31; 6:4).

The ancient world was a man's world. Nowhere was this more true than at home. The Jews related to their wives as little more than replaceable personal property. The Greeks restricted their women to the women's own quarters and did not so much as allow the women to eat meals with the men. Paul speaks against the status quo of his days, pointing out a more responsible and involved role for the men of his time and certainly for the *Men for These Times*.[1]

Paul suggests that husbands should love their wives as Christ loved the church. To be sure, a true husband is one who nurtures and cares for his wife by relating to her as a partner instead of treating her like someone under his control. A true husband will properly provide for his wife (see 1 Timothy 5:8). The wife working outside the home does not lessen the husband's God-given responsibilities to support his wife and children.

The supreme test of loving one's wife as Christ loved the church would be to give up personal pleasure for her happiness. Perhaps this may mean watching less *Monday Night*

Football and spending more time talking about important family matters. The pleasures to give up will differ from man to man. However, the notion of giving up personal pleasure for the happiness of one's spouse begins to approximate, in a very small way, Christ's love for the church.

Paul counsels men to love their wives as they love their own bodies. God's own pronouncement in Genesis 2:24 is that marriage makes husband and wife "one flesh." Such an abstraction should direct men to affirm their wives as individuals instead of physically or emotionally abusing them; for when a man abuses his wife, he in essence abuses himself, a matter that too frequently takes place among those who profess to be Christians.

The oneness of husband and wife presented in the Pauline writings implies that husband and wife share ideals, goals, and spiritual values. Consequently, when she succeeds, he succeeds; when she is happy, he is happy.[2]

A few years ago, after finishing course work for a Ph.D. in sociology and feeling frustrated by the fact that my advisor had retired and moved to the other end of the country, leaving me with an almost impossible situation to ever complete my program, I told my wife it was her turn. Elaine and I had agreed that after a certain number of years in my doctoral program, it would be her turn to go to graduate school. Elaine was accepted into the graduate school of her choice; and as I had done, she worked full time and studied full time. We lived in the New York City area at the time, and Elaine had a daily two-hour commute on the Long Island Railroad. So I got to pick up the kids, supervise homework, cook dinner, give baths, have worship, read stories, and put Jessica and Julian to bed four or five days a week during a two-year period.

I could not begin to tell you how the Lord helped us during this time. I had to do all of this in addition to my fifty- to sixty-hour work week as a conference departmental director. There was no one happier than I, however, when the children and I attended Elaine's graduation and watched her get her master's degree. I was so proud of my wife; that was also my degree. Elaine was successful, and that made me successful. She was happy, and that made me happy. Oneness. It has to be more than just a biblical notion; it must take shape in the daily routine of our lives.

In his counsel to fathers, which in a broader sense also includes mothers, Paul cautions us not to provoke our children. In other words, not to anger, enrage, infuriate, irritate, vex, nettle, roil, peeve, or annoy them, if the obedience required is to be obtained for the right reasons. The lack of respect for parents today often is a result of unjust, and sometimes brutal and inconsistent, demands made by parents on children. In these cases, even though outward obedience may be achieved by violent means, it is at the expense of honor and respect.

One author wrote: "Fathers, ... combine affection with authority, kindness and sympathy with firm restraint. Give some of your leisure hours to your children; become acquainted with them; associate with them in their work and in their sports, and win their confidence. Cultivate friendship with them, especially your sons. In this way you will be a strong influence for good."[3]

Dad just died seven months ago. However, he left his

legacy with me, which I hope to pass on to Julian, my son. If this kind of father image has not been a part of your experience, I urge you to turn to our heavenly Father, who has promised to supply all our needs. God can make you the man, husband, and/or father you need to be.

1. Curtis Vaughan, *Ephesians* (Grand Rapids, Mich.: Zondervan Publishing House, 1977), 117.
2. *The Seventh-day Adventist Bible Commentary* (revised edition) (Hagerstown, Md.: Review and Herald Publishing Association, 1980), 6:1037.
3. Ellen G. White, *The Adventist Home* (Nashville: Southern Publishing Association, 1952), 222.

Willie Oliver is the family ministries director of the North American Division. He has written for various publications, including *Celebration* and *Insight*. He is a member of the American Sociological Association, the Black Adventist Youth Directors Association, and the New York Academy of Sciences. He completed his Ph.D. in sociology at Columbia University in New York City.

That ugly word divorce *is ripping families apart. What happens when it invades your home? When you wake up one morning and realize that you've lost it all?*

———

Portrait of a Divorced Daddy

by Robert J. Walker

I never thought it would happen to me. But, in spite of all my education and personal and religious convictions, there I was, sitting in the lawyer's office discussing how the assets of my eight-year marriage would be divided. She got the house and all the furnishings, the car, and custody of the most important, precious, and best thing that came out of the marriage—our then-five-year-old son, Cedric.

I was left with a handsome child support payment, all the medical expenses of my son, and the task of repaying the debts we had accumulated over the duration of the marriage. By the time I left the lawyer's office, the only property I owned was my truck and personal clothing.

After the divorce, I quickly began to realize that one of the most difficult things to cope with was the loss of time with my son.

I would no longer be there each night to read him a Bible

story and to tuck him in bed with his favorite teddy bear. I would no longer be there each night to pray with him and to hear that sweet child's voice say, ". . . and God please bless Mommy and Daddy and Grand-mommy, and help me to be a good little boy. Amen."

I would no longer be there to get a good-night kiss and to hear him say, as he fell asleep, "Daddy, I love you!" Nor would I have the privilege of responding, "I love you too, Cedric."

There are so many other things I miss. I miss being there to take him to meet his new teacher on the first day of school. I miss being there to help him with his homework. I miss our going outside in the yard to play catch or fixing him a peanut-butter-and-jelly sandwich. I miss being there to place a Band-Aid on a cut. I miss being there to establish the Little League baseball and basketball teams that I promised him I would organize when he turned nine.

When Cedric was six years old, I went to a thrift shop and bought some Little League baseball and basketball uniforms. He would sleep in one of the basketball uniforms, even though it was too big for him. His favorite uniform was number 23 (Michael Jordan's original number).

Even now when we talk on the phone and when we are together, he reminds me of my promising him to start the teams, or else he mentions how someone at church was talking about organizing the teams, but no one seems to have the time.

So much of the literature today talks about the hurt that women go through as a result of a divorce. Well, men hurt too. Not only do we have to deal with the stigma of being divorced and with friends and church members naturally assuming the failure was all the man's fault, but often we are the one who lose custody of the children.

I was prepared mentally to deal with the financial burdens of the divorce. I was also prepared to deal with the scorn and separation I would receive from church members and friends. However, I was not prepared to deal with the tears that fill my son's eyes when we have had time together, and it is time for me to take him home.

I was not prepared to deal with the loneliness I would feel when I would see how he looked as I got into my truck to make the five-hour trip back to Alabama. I was not prepared to deal with the many times I, even now, look at his picture and wish he were here with me.

Even after five years of divorce, it still hurts. All children need both parents. But a boy especially needs his daddy.

My ex-wife remarried and ended all hopes of the family being reunited. My son's stepdaddy seems to be a nice guy. But there is no substitute for the natural father. Through this unhappy event in my life, I now have a better understanding of the awesome sacrifice that was made for my salvation. I now have a better understanding of how God must have felt when He was separated from His Son Jesus, whom He allowed to come to this earth and give His life for our sins.

Robert J. Walker is a college professor in the Department of Education at Oakwood College.

A young father begins to grasp the simplest concepts of Christianity when he realizes that the best thing anyone could do for him is to be kind to his daughter.

———

My Daughter's Gift

by Russ Hall

As a man, I suppose I have the same thoughts and feelings that all men have. Some are noble and good, while others are vile products of the sinful nature that leap uninvited into the thought process and must be expelled when they are recognized for what they are.

I have lived my life, for the most part, trying to accentuate the good tendencies I see in myself and weed out the bad, though sometimes events in life expose character flaws that I had previously been unaware of.

Not until my daughter came into my life did I begin to grasp one of the simplest concepts of Christian behavior, and from a viewpoint that I never would have had, had it not been for her.

She is four now. Kind and gentle as my wife—just as we have taught her to be. She is my greatest joy. As I watch her grow and encounter an ever-increasing circle of people, it occurs to me that the best thing anyone could ever do for me is to be kind to her. The deepest pain I can imagine would be to see her suffer mistreatment.

As human beings, we sometimes tend not to treat others as we should. If people annoy or provoke us, retaliation is our first thought. Of this I am guilty. Even though I never have been a really mean person, I have treated those who made me angry as though I didn't care about them. Then love for my daughter began to change my outlook.

Who among us would not be greatly embarrassed and feel crushing guilt to discover that we had mistreated another, only to learn that the person whom we wronged was the child of our closest friend? Who could mistreat the children of a father who loves them as much as I love my daughter and still hope to remain his friend?

I can't always watch over my daughter. As she grows, she will spend more time away from me. She will encounter other people, some of whom will be stronger, smarter, and more worldly than she is. Some will be cunning and cruel. The world will not always be kind to her. I feel a father's regret, because I know now what she will find out later, when the innocence of childhood meets the deceits of the world.

But as for me, my little girl has given me a great gift. My eyes can see people as I never could have seen them before. Now, when conflicts arise with others, instead of lashing out at people as though they were worthless, I try to look closely at each one and say to myself, "I won't let you make me mistreat you, because I know your Father. He's my best friend, and He came and found me when I was lost."

———————————

Russ Hall is a sign designer for Wesco, Inc. He and his wife and little girl live in China Grove, North Carolina.

A father's love to his prodigal daughter.

———

A Love Letter to My Daughter

by Salim Hasbani

I have made several attempts to write you, but every time I've had to abandon the task simply because I wasn't able to find the words to express what was in my heart.

I have loved you since you were a tiny baby. Nothing can change my love, no matter what mistakes you've made or successes you've achieved. My love to you, like God's love to us, cannot be defeated or altered by any circumstances. God calls it an everlasting love. It lasts forever, and forever means until one of us ceases to exist. Yet even then, the wonderful memories we have of the other will last till the end of time.

I miss you terribly, and I'm having a hard time coping. You'll always be my little girl. On the other hand, that same love demands that after a certain age, I have to set you free. They call it cutting off the apron strings. They also call it tough love. You are an adult now, and adulthood requires independence. To be allowed to make your own decisions and therefore reap the rewards of your good decisions, as well as pay the penalty of your wrong ones.

For reasons I can only guess, you've exercised that freedom to cut your ties with your church and with your family. I have to talk to you like an adult. If guilt, shame, or any other cause separates you from those who truly love you, take heart. We've all done something in our past to be ashamed of. I've done things that I will regret all my life. I've had to ask God to forgive me and, above all, forgive myself. I figured that life is too short to go around carrying excess baggage.

God has given you a vibrant and beautiful personality. You have tremendous potential. You are young, and the best of your life is still ahead of you. It is never too late. The Bible tells us that with God, all things are possible.

I'd like to invite you to pick up the remnant pieces of your life. Painstakingly arrange the pieces in a pattern, and make God the centerpiece. Life is never easy. We all know that nobody promised us a bed of roses. Rain must fall in every life, for without rain flowers never grow.

Sooner or later, all of us will have a time of need. Please allow those who love you the opportunity to be there during your time of need. And I want you to be there for me as I am here for you today.

Please forgive me if I have hurt you in any way, and allow us to have the joy of sharing with you the few years left for both of us.

Write me, or call. I long to hear from you.

I love you with all my heart and always will.

Your dad,

Salim Hasbani writes from Bakersfield, California, where he works in administration at a government hospital.

What do you do when your business takes you away from home so much that your children treat you as a guest? A former businessman discusses decisions with consequences.

The Handshake and the Diaper

by Keavin Hayden

It was truly a morning of sweaty palms and tensed nerves. I was on my way to meet the vice-president of sales and marketing of my company, who had flown all the way across country to meet with me. I guess he wanted to find out firsthand why a young corporate manager would suddenly resign just after being promoted to a new management position, a position for which I had worked hard.

As I drove to the hotel, I rehearsed what I was going to say. My motivation to quit, stemmed from several deep convictions. Since becoming a Christian, my priorities in life seemed to be shifting. I could already see that excelling in my business career would not allow me time to develop the relationship I desired with my young family. It often pained me to say goodbye for days at a time and then be greeted as a guest by the children when I arrived home. They needed me more than that.

Also, although I couldn't explain it, I felt as though God was calling me from the prosperous business world to do something in His work. Anyway, I had already made the difficult decision to quit, even though I didn't know where I was going to go or what I was going to do. I simply placed my trust in the God of Abraham and responded to my heavenly Father's call to leave my earthly occupational security.

I sometimes wonder if scenes such as the one that took place that morning in Teaneck, New Jersey, were what the apostle was trying to describe when he wrote, "Those who have bought into this world's philosophy see the preaching of the cross as foolishness. But we who know the meaning of Calvary have experienced its influence in our lives, and we know it to be the power of God" (1 Corinthians 1:18, *The Clear Word Bible*).

Truly, the vice-president who listened to me that morning thought I was foolish, as did many of my family members and friends. But I gained courage as I read "in all fields, nigh and afar off, men will be called from the plow and from the more common commercial business vocations that largely occupy the mind, and will be educated in connection with men of experience. As they learn to labor effectively they will proclaim the truth with power."*

What a promising thought and ultimate privilege! God using ordinary humanity to finish the gospel work. I wanted to be one of those men, yet little did I realize what preparatory education lay ahead for me as I walked out of the hotel room that early summer morning.

You must understand, I had convinced myself that in

leaving such a prestigious and financially lucrative job as I had, God would reward me with something comparable in His work. I was ready to do something big! Yet the trade-off was anything but what I expected. Instead of a healthy regular paycheck, I received poverty and debt. In place of exercising my sales skills each day, I was confronted with perplexities I had never known before, such as plumbing, carpentry, and scouting around for odd jobs. My hand, which had become used to beginning each business day with an important handshake, was now handed a diaper by an overtaxed wife. I began noticing that I was always telling people what I used to be. That bothered me a lot. What had happened? Was I not usable material for God? Had I made a wrong decision? I often cried myself into a desperate sleep, which seemed to be my only relief.

Then God began to teach me valuable lessons, which I am still learning. Through the life story of Moses, I discovered that we sometimes err by laying out our own plans of work to do for the Lord and then running headstrong toward them. And as God did with Moses, He must let us over and over again prove ourselves miserable failures in carrying out our ideas and plans. Humility is not an easy achievement. Dying to our self-important egos is like circumcision at thirty. It hurts! Yet if we fail to learn it, we will render ourselves unusable to God when His cause will need us most.

I have come to realize that the race for eternal life is run on a path strewn with land mines. Continuously we encounter dangerous detours that appeal to our human reasoning. God is forever trying to teach us that the right decisions are in most cases unpopular because His ways are not man's ways. And in this race, decisions determine eternity.

The development of a personal relationship with Jesus Christ is mandatory for making right decisions in our Christian experience. Only as we come to know the Master, how He reasons, and what His desires and purposes are, will we ever be equipped to successfully implement His plans for our lives. We must do things His way, not ours. And we can only understand His way by habitually communing with Him in private prayer, Bible study, and working together with Him for souls. Every decision we make, however small, should be made in light of the revelation of His plans for our lives.

Often we must choose between two *good* or otherwise *right* options. Sometimes it simply is a matter of prioritizing those options. I personally experienced this shortly after leaving my job. My focus was entirely on how God was going to use me in a big way in what I considered His work. My wife consistently told me that the training of my children would prove to be my highest calling in this life. That's what the diaper was all about. But this seemed to me to be a roadblock to my giant ideas.

Then I began to understand more of Jesus. He could have evangelized the entire world with His first visit. Instead, He focused on discipling twelve. Somehow God began to reveal to me that if I would properly disciple my little flock at home, heaven would record this as a great accomplishment.

Prioritizing decisions is nothing new. Eli labored much

for God but lost his sons and dishonored his Redeemer in the process. Zechariah and Elizabeth, on the other hand, left the temple service to quietly raise their boy in the obscurity of the wilderness. The result of such a decision stands on record through the life of John the Baptist.

Striking a balance is essential for us fathers who have a yearning burden to labor in fields that extend outside our homes. The training of children and being a part of the church's work in spreading the gospel are not incompatible. And we will only be satisfied as we successfully accomplish both.

There is no question that properly training our children must come first, for they are the future church. But as I have prayerfully watched, I have found that a great portion of that training can be incorporated into laboring for others. After all, isn't that what we are training them for, to toil to save those who are lost? If we were as eager to get our children involved in our missionary activities as in the things of this world, such as rivalry sports and worldly amusement, I believe we would begin to see things as God sees them. These other things will never yield our youth eternal results or even a sense of satisfaction in this life. But let a young person be involved in winning a soul for the kingdom, and he or she is hooked for life.

I once heard a preacher say that we should pray that the Holy Spirit would turn our young people loose. I believe that we, their parents, are the ones that need to turn them loose by the example of the priorities in our own lives. Most likely, they will copy our pattern. And when they someday understand the hard and unpopular decisions we have

made in order to train them to save souls, then they will be
better equipped to understand the love of God that was
expressed through His decision to send His Son to save us.

* Ellen G. White, *Testimonies for the Church*, 9:96.

Keavin Hayden is the author of *The Shaking Among
God's People,* published by the Review and Herald.
He is a self-supporting lay evangelist who lives on
a farm in northwest Arkansas with his wife and
three children.

Section 6

The Best That I Can Be

Continue to work out your salvation with fear and trembling, for it is God who works in you to will and to act according to his good purpose. . . . So that you may become blameless and pure, children of God without fault in a crooked and depraved generation, in which you shine like stars in the universe.

Philippians 2:12, 15.

The Caring Male

by Joseph Leininger Wheeler

Thank heaven for women's lib! That may sound like a strange thing to say . . . but there are reasons why I say it. Women weren't the only ones locked into their claustrophobic stereotypes. As late as my own childhood, I remember hearing and seeing the polarized male/female roles played out from day to day.

Mother was the soft one, the one who would respond to tears, to entreaties, to sob stories. Dad was the tough one, apparently impervious to all of the above: if I cried, he would merely lay it on harder in order to give me "something to cry for."

One was made to fear one's father in those days: "Just wait until your FATHER comes home" sent chills up every child's spine—especially every boy's. One's only hope was that somehow, some way, Mother could be dissuaded from telling the story to Father, for it was a foregone conclusion what would happen once she did: the woodshed, the switch, the belt.

Yet, in all fairness, I can't really blame my father: he was merely disciplining me in the same way his father had disciplined him, and in turn his father had disciplined the same way by Grandfather, and so on, back as far as anyone could remember. Not only that, but when I was growing up, all my male friends "got it" just as regularly as I did. We expected it: it had apparently always been that way, and there seemed precious little likelihood that it would change.

And then came women's lib. When women belatedly began shattering their shells of subservience, they initiated a process that none of them even dreamed of: the masculinization of women and the feminization of men; the building up of the woman's self-esteem and the tearing down of the man's. For as woman began to find herself at long last, to live out her dream, the husband lost the full-time support system at home, and the son lost the full-time mother. Thus males were dealt a double-whammy. Women, on the other hand, in order to survive in the career jungle, were forced to develop a militant role—and that had heretofore been considered a male preserve.

But, on the distaff, neither was all bad, for woman had become so ethereal, so otherworldly and spiritlike—so delicate that she fainted at the slightest pretext—that man had lost respect for her mind and had learned to walk all over her. Man, on the other hand, had become so brutal, stoical, unimaginative, and unresponsive that he had almost lost whatever sensitivity the race had ever had. He was locked into an iron mask: a man never cried, never showed emotion—in short, he bottled it in and bottled it in, until a coronary blew his cardiovascular cork.

It is not my purpose to worry much about how far the pendulum may swing. The significant thing is that not even "all the King's horses and all the King's men" could possibly ever put Humpty Dumpty back on his Maginot wall. That was a world we will never see again.

In reality, there have always been dominant women and subservient men—it is just that society viewed them as misfit failures. Women's lib has inadvertently given both of them credibility.

No longer is it invariably, "Wait till your FATHER gets home!" It is no longer uncommon for father and child to wait for MOTHER to come home. Each individual has been freed to follow his or her own path, rather than a standardized one.

So it has come to pass that the male can care, can love, can minister, can be sensitive, can be empathetic, can be solicitous. Can be loved instead of feared. What a revolutionary change that is!

And how very much the caring male is needed. Today, Mother—due to full-time jobs at both home and office—is unlikely to have much ministering energy left at the end of the day. The man—partly due to his bull-headed refusal to assume his fair share of the household load—is actually likely to have more time than his wife to minister!

Sitting next to me on a long transcontinental flight was a weary young woman returning to husband and child after having left Europe forty-eight sleepless hours earlier.

Seeing how utterly exhausted she was, I stood up, pulled a pillow and blanket out of the overhead compartment, handed them to her, pulled up the middle seat arm, and suggested she stretch out and take a nap.

Half a year later, I received a letter. It was postmarked Salt Lake City, and in it my erstwhile seatmate thanked me for—in her words—"being kind." What struck me about her going to all this trouble to unearth my address and write me was this: If a simple act of kindness by a stranger meant this much, then that ingredient must be in awfully short supply in this nation today!

The telephone rang at my desk in Thousand Oaks, California, a few years ago. On the line was a woman I hadn't seen since I taught her in school twenty years earlier. She asked if I couldn't somehow make it to her twentieth class reunion in Sacramento the following day. Now, it's a long way from L.A. to Sacramento; furthermore, we had eight people invited for lunch the next day, so I reluctantly turned her down. After I hung up, however, I called my wife and told her I didn't feel at all good about turning her down. "Well," she responded, "if you feel that strongly about it, we can always uninvite the eight people and go."

We arrived at a Sacramento motel in the wee hours of the morning. The next day was one long love fest. Late that night, adieus were at last being made, with everyone hugging and crying and no one wanting to leave first. Just before we left, the woman who had called me asked me a question: "Would you like to know why we went to so much trouble to get you here?"

The Caring Male

"Of course I would," I responded.

Never, in a million years, could I have guessed her answer. The reason she went to so much trouble to track me down had virtually nothing to do with my teaching expertise, my testing, my bulletin boards, my daily sayings on the blackboard, my involvement in extracurricular activities, my paperback library campaigns, my wacky sense of humor. No, the reason she went to so much trouble to find me was that during a discussion with classmates about which teacher they'd most like to have with them, in discussing me, two simple acts of kindness they remembered tipped the balance my way.

I have never been able to get over it. That experience radically changed my life's priorities. I am now convinced that kindness is one most crucial character trait in God's universe: one that embodies, and is distilled from, all the other character traits God expects us to have and develop.

I submit that it is virtually impossible to be a caring, loving person without also being kind. Without that vital ingredient, love is not love at all, but sadistic egocentricity. One can't flee farther from the heart of God than to that icy island called "Cruelty." Farther from God, in fact, than that equally frigid land called "Pride."

This being so, and it being so easy to be kind, one would naturally expect the world to be awash with kindness. Tragically, the reverse is true: kindness is seemingly one of the scarcest attributes on this troubled planet.

It used to be almost axiomatic that kindness was an attribute women were expected to have but that was merely an option for men. Today, however, all too often, kindness

129

has degenerated into being merely an option for women—which obviously means that if the male sex does not take up the slack, it is going to be in very short supply!

It is long past time for men to conquer their fear of the New Woman and put their own house in order. Paradoxically, only as males stiffen their backbones and assume their God-given roles as father, husband, brother, uncle, grandfather, cousin, godfather, mentor, and friend will women respect them and there be any real chance for the family, as we have known it in the past, to continue to exist.

Kindness unaccompanied by strength is not kindness at all, but merely weakness. Kindness, by its very nature, cannot flow out of an empty chamber. Weakness is an empty chamber. No one ever goes to a weak person for help, for solace, for counsel, or even for a long-term relationship.

Only a strong, caring man can hold a strong woman for long.

Sometimes kindness is endowed by one's genes at birth. For others, kindness is a learned virtue—often the byproduct of trauma, troubles, and tribulations.

Permit me the use of a tree metaphor. In a verdant valley, in a hollow protected from the wind, stands a tall, stately poplar, blessed with roots that extend just far enough downward to keep it erect. In the absence of any kind of atmospheric stress, that is all it needs. High above it, on a mountain's crest, is a storm-battered oak. In order to survive, it has clawed it root ends deep into soil and rock. Thus a hurricane can do its worst, yet the oak still stands.

When we are assailed by the troubles of life, where will

we go for the courage to fight on? Most certainly not to the untried poplar with its shallow roots! Rather, we will make the trek to the triumphant oak on the cliff's edge.

Christ is such an oak—that is why, during His earthly ministry, pain-racked men and women reached out, even in the press of huge crowds, to but touch the garment He wore, in hopes that some of that power would arc from the Master into them. That it actually did is manifested by Christ's stopping, in the middle of jostling people, to ask the ostensibly ridiculous question: "Who touched Me?"

While none of us is divine, yet we may share, through our relationship with the Master, in His strength. When that occurs, people will surround us, seeking to touch our garments. Thus, we have the opportunity to be a partner with God in ministering to His lambs.

Joseph L. Wheeler chairs the English Department at Columbia Union College in Takoma Park, Maryland. His books include *Christmas in My Heart*, volumes 1, 2, 3, and 4; *Remote Controlled*; and *View at Your Own Risk*.

—

The Man Who
Influenced Me Most

by Zane Grey

(Supplied by Joseph L. Wheeler)

Note: The following is an example of how one man can touch the lives of many. It was taken from the history of the American West. The frontier writer Zane Grey first met him in 1907, in a Flagstaff, Arizona, courtroom. Later on, Jim Emett (elsewhere spelled Emmett) accompanied legendary frontiersman Buffalo Jones and Grey's party by wagon train to Emett's paradise on the Colorado River, Lee's Ferry. Emett subsequently accompanied Jones and Grey on two mountain lion–lassoing expeditions, later immortalized as *Last of the Plainsmen* and *Roping Lions in the Grand Canyon*. Even more significant, however, is a book some consider to be one of the greatest westerns ever written, *Heritage of the Desert* (Harper, 1910). Grey's protagonist was named August Naab—and Naab is one of the most towering titans in all American literature. In real life, August Naab was Jim Emett: lock, stock, and barrel.

The Man Who Influenced Me Most

Almost twenty years later, Grey wrote these words about Emett:

This home of Emett's was a hundred sixty miles from Flagstaff, and about as far in the other direction from any settlement. His only neighbors were Navajo Indians, and they lived far across the river, beyond the saw-toothed Echo cliffs.

Jim Emett had been married twice and had eighteen children. His present wife was a comely, ruddy-faced woman, sweet-voiced and merry, always busy and happy. . . .

It was wonderful to see the children flock after Jim Emett and climb over him if he chanced to sit down. Sometimes they would remind me of Gulliver and his pygmies. That Jim Emett had a great heart then became as manifest as his giant form. I saw five tots swing from his outstretched brawny arm.

I tramped around the oasis with Emett, gauging for myself the evidences of his superhuman labors and listening to the simple, enthralling narratives of which he had such store. His work had kept him out upon the open desert ranges, where the cattle ran, or up on the high plateau, where the sheep grazed. Yet during the years there at Lee's Ferry he had built up a monument of labor that seemed incredible as the prowess of one man. You had only to look at his hands, however, to believe him capable of any physical task. They were huge and brawny, yet remarkably mobile and deft despite the horny palms and calloused fingers.

Emett was a splendid carpenter, as the cabins, sheds,

and homemade furniture attested. He also made all the harnesses, from the tanning of his hides to the forging of buckles. He was a capital blacksmith. I saw him pound out a horseshoe from a straight bar of iron. Many were the proofs of his capacity as a mason, especially the smooth hearth, the splendidly drawing open fireplaces, the stone chimneys, and particularly the tunnel piercing a corner of cliff through which he had drawn Pariah Creek to irrigate the oasis. The orchards and fields of alfalfa, the grapevines that Jones averred grew bunches of incredible size, the pumpkins so big I could not roll one over, the intensive cultivation of the rich, red soil—these things were proof of Emett's prowess as a farmer. . . .

Any visitor at Lee's Ferry would have been struck with the variety of pets that overran the place. Dogs, rabbits, burros, a deer, a coyote, two foxes, squirrels, cats, and quail, lambs and rams, colts and horses, all mingled together with the children in a lazy, drowsy, contented life, characteristic of Emett's household. A more careful search discovered different kinds of birds that made their homes in the cottonwoods.

Emett had at one time and another collected this menagerie. Anything crippled, hurt, lost, deserted, or sick found refuge with Jim Emett. He loved and cared for all these creatures as he did the children. Marvelous indeed how he ever found time for all! But he did. The earliest streak of gray dawn in the east found this desert man at his many tasks.

They told me that Emett's mercy and protection extended to outcast and starved Indians, to wanderers of the wasteland who happened by the Ferry, to cowboys and sheep-herders out of jobs. His gate was ever open. Rustlers and horse thieves, outlaws from the noted Hole in the Wall, an isolated rendezvous back in the canyon, hunted fugitives—all were welcomed by Jim Emett. He had no fear of any man. He feared only his God.

The impact Emett had on Zane Grey can be the impact each strong, caring man has on all those whose lives intersect with his from day to day:

I had to revere him. I had to love him. And, in as much as was possible for me, I gritted my teeth and began the development of endurance. It sustained me through years of defeat, of deferred longing and labor, when otherwise I would have fallen by the wayside. To seek, to strive, to find, and not to yield, these hands that forged the strong soul of Ulysses were assuredly the strength of Jim Emett (quoted from Zane Grey, "The Man Who Influenced Me Most," *American Magazine*, August 1926).

Joe Wheeler is an authority on the life of Zane Grey and is the executive director of Zane Grey's West Society.

Does your life seem like one crisis after another? Then you have much in common with Adventist pioneer Uriah Smith, who experienced numerous crises. A look at how this Review *editor dealt with his difficulties should help us handle our own.*

And So Can You

by Eugene F. Durand

Have you ever felt bitterly disappointed in God or the church? Young Uriah was baptized as an Adventist in the summer of 1844 at the age of twelve and proclaimed to his neighbors that the Lord was coming on October 22. When the advent failed to materialize, he put religion on the "back burner" during his adolescent years. But the setback proved only temporary, for he spent the last fifty years of his life preaching the Lord's soon coming. He bounced back, and so can you.

Has your life been plagued by some physical problem? Shortly after the Great Disappointment, twelve-year-old Uriah had his infected left leg amputated, the operation being performed on the kitchen table without anesthetic. For the rest of his life, he walked on a wooden leg, which led to a sedentary life that contributed to later illness. But it also contributed to greater development of his literary, artistic, and inventive talents. He made "lemonade" out of his "lemon," and so can you.

Have you ever had to choose between God and Mammon? At age twenty Uriah Smith planned to enter Harvard and prepare for a teaching career. But when he heard James and Ellen White explain the Sabbath and the reason for the Disappointment, he studied the matter and cast his lot with the remnant. As in Jesus' life, baptism was followed by a great temptation. One month later, he and his sister Annie received an offer to take charge of a new academy at three times the salary he would work up to eight years later as editor of *The Advent Review and Sabbath Herald*. But they turned it down to work at the *Review* for room and board only. He made the right choice, and so can you.

Are you being worked to a frazzle? Ten years of editing the church paper left Brother Smith ready for a breakdown. As a result, he and four other church leaders went to Dr. Jackson's Dansville, New York, health institution to recuperate. The church devoted four days to fasting and prayer for them. After resting his weary body and brain for twelve weeks, a rejuvenated editor returned to the task and kept at it with but two brief breaks until he "died with his boots on" at age seventy. He learned how to slow down, and so can you.

Do you ever feel like a failure? Recognizing the need for another break four years later, the *Review* editor left his office to work as an engraver for ten months. When James White asked why he hadn't returned after six months, Smith replied that he deemed himself unworthy to work for the church any longer, owing to "past failures" in the financial management of the paper. Others encouraged him to return, however, and he did so, willing to serve as best he could. He overcame discouragement, and so can you.

Have you ever lost your job? After twenty years with the *Review*, Uriah Smith was fired. Apparently he had come into conflict with James and Ellen White over how to run the church paper. Moving to Grand Rapids, he again worked at engraving, earning twice his editorial salary. After six months, however, he saw his error and came into full harmony with his co-workers. Restored to his position, he held it for thirty more years. He learned from his hard experience, and so can you.

Have you ever had to resign a position because of sharp disagreements? Nine years later, Elder Smith became involved in a controversy over educational policies that led him to resign as chairman of the board of Battle Creek College. The school closed down for a year. He disagreed with Professor Goodloe Bell and refused to accept Ellen White's rebukes regarding his own actions. But in time, the elder accepted the prophetic messages as true and sought Bell's forgiveness. He found a way to settle disagreements, and so can you.

Do you sometimes clash with others over theology? When E. J. Waggoner and A. T. Jones presented their emphasis on righteousness by faith at the 1888 General Conference session in Minneapolis, Uriah Smith opposed them. He felt that their position would undermine the Seventh-day Adventist message on the importance of the law. When

Ellen White appealed to him, he made a public confession of his wrong attitude toward her as well as toward Jones and Waggoner. Although he later revived the controversy in the *Review*, he then served amicably under Jones's editorship for four years and retained great admiration for Ellen White. He could disagree without being disagreeable, and so can you.

Has someone else gotten a position you felt you should have? During the last year of Uriah Smith's life, W. W. Prescott was appointed as *Review* editor. Although the veteran had served the paper for nearly fifty years and had been the one who encouraged the younger man to enter church work, he hid this final great disappointment and upheld the new editor, doing all in his power to facilitate a smooth transition, thus earning Prescott's enduring gratitude. He knew how to step aside gracefully, and so can you.

For half a century, Uriah Smith proved faithful to the cause of God. To you he wrote:

O Brother be faithful: soon Jesus will come,
For whom we have waited so long;
O soon shall we enter our glorious home,
And join in the conqueror's song.

Eugene F. Durand recently retired after eighteen years on the editorial staff of the *Adventist Review*. Previously he served as a pastor, missionary, and teacher. He holds a Ph.D. in American Religious History, with his dissertation resulting in the book

Yours in the Blessed Hope, Uriah Smith, on which this piece is based.

Have you ever felt totally worthless? This author lived in the ghettos of Brooklyn, New York. Despised and spat at, he strove in vain to prove himself.

———

How Much Are You Worth?

by Louis Torres

I was walking down the street in Brooklyn when a man approached me from the opposite direction. As he met up with me, he turned, spat at my feet, and said, "Why don't you go back where you came from?" It made me feel as though I was worthless and that my worth amounted to nothing more than spit. This began a series of complexes in my life that compelled me to find ways of increasing my worth.

I was only ten years old at the time, but lack of self-esteem is no respecter of persons. So I ventured on my quest. How could I add worth to myself?

Watching television and seeing the *Little Rascals*, the idea came to me that if I could just become like one of those young boys, I could be worth something. I went to my mother's cupboards and pulled out a can of lard. I pasted it on my hair, combed it into the style of Alfalfa, and then went outside. My hopes shattered as the kids laughed at me and the girls, holding their noses, responded, "You stink!"

Oh, if only I could be Jewish or Italian! So I made an attempt to appear like Sal Armenio, who was a famous movie star at the time. I combed my hair like Sal and tried to lift up my lip to appear as sexy as he did. I practiced for hours, days, until finally I accomplished the feat. In fact, I can still lift up my lip, but to my discouragement, I still lacked self-worth.

I realize now that I was like many other men who try various strategies for strengthening their self-esteem. They seek to prove they are somebody by prowling around in a car with a beautiful woman or by sex or by how much money they have or by how strong they are. Some depend on their house or position at work.

Just how much are you worth? The Bible says in 1 Corinthians 6:20, "Ye are bought with a price" (KJV). God has paid a price to purchase us, to redeem us, to reclaim us. But what is that price? "Forasmuch as ye know that ye were not redeemed with corruptible things, as silver and gold, from your vain conversation received by tradition from your fathers; but with the precious blood of Christ, as of a lamb without blemish and without spot" (1 Peter 1:18, 19, KJV).

Think of it! God could have used gold or silver, but He thought our worth greater and could think of nothing better to demonstrate how priceless we are than to offer the blood of His own Son. God established our value.

But, you may ask, "What is it about me that is worth that much?"

Every individual on planet Earth is unique. There is not another one like you or me in the whole world! There are people who may have our same name or who may resemble us in some way. But there is not another person exactly like you. God only made one of you, and when there is only one of a kind, it is priceless.

I was visiting Canada and decided to enroll in the frequent flyer program. I approached the counter and gave the woman my name. "Your name is already here," she said.

"No, that's impossible. I've never registered," I told her.

"Well, it's your name."

"It may be my name, but it's not me," I replied. Then I gave her my address. Eleven Louis Torreses showed up on the computer screen! Eleven Louis Torreses, but not one of them was me. Many people all around the world may look or talk or walk just like me, but I am the only one who has ever had the experiences that I have gone through. I am the only one born of my mother and father, the only one who has had all my brothers, sisters, relatives. I am unique. God made only one of me, and because I am one of a kind, I am priceless. So are you. We have a special place in God's heart, and no one will ever be able to take that place.

I grew up in Brooklyn, New York, in the ghettos. My mother raised all six of us boys by herself. But one brother was always in trouble. My mother wept and pleaded with him. She whipped him. She talked with him, but nothing worked. He was sent to reform school, but when he came out, he went right back to his old lifestyle. Poor Mother would stay up until the early hours of the morning, waiting for him to come home. Killing herself with love for him.

Then he landed in prison. We begged her to forget him, but she could not. She'd wake up early in the morning to prepare food for him, then ride treacherous subways, buses, and the ferry to see him.

One New Year's Eve, we were together, the five of us boys with our wives and children, waiting for midnight to strike in Times Square. As the hour struck, we began to rejoice, typical of our family practice on that night. I went to embrace my mother, but I couldn't find her in the crowd. As I looked for her, I heard the sound of crying in a bedroom. There she was, sobbing for our wayward brother.

Somewhat irritated, I said, "Mother, what's wrong with you? Aren't five of us enough for you?"

With tears streaming down her face, she looked at me and said, "Son, I want to say something to you that I hope you will never forget. Each one of you has a special place in my heart."

If my mother, with all her sins and frailties and weaknesses, could have a special place in her heart for each one of us, then what about the One who made Mother's heart? Yes, you and I have a special place in His heart. When He died on Calvary, He had you on His mind.

No longer do we have to seek to prove our standing with others. No longer do we have to strive for ascendancy. No longer do we have to be in bondage with complexes, feeling inferior. No, our worth has been established on Calvary.

How Much Are You Worth?

Thank God for your worth!

Louis Torres is the director of lay evangelism at *Amazing Facts*. He also worked with the North American Division and Media Center, training laypeople for Net 95.

"He has the sensitivity of a frog" seems to be the latest pet phrase in the female repertoire. Are they talking about you?

———

The Power of Sensitivity

by Delbert W. Baker

Sensitivity has a power and effectiveness like few other personality traits. In his book *Weathering the Storm*, Dan Clark illustrates the need for sensitivity even in the little areas of life. A store owner was tacking a sign above his door that read "Puppies for Sale." Signs like that attract children, and sure enough, a little boy appeared under the store owner's sign. "How much are you going to sell the puppies for?" he asked.

The store owner replied, "Anywhere from $30 to $50."

The little boy reached in his pocket and pulled out some coins. "I have some change. I have $2.37," he said. "Can I please look at them?"

The store owner smiled and whistled. Out of the kennel came Lady, who ran down the aisle of his store, followed by five teeny, tiny balls of fur. One puppy was lagging considerably behind. Immediately, the little boy singled out the lagging, limping puppy and asked, "What's wrong with that little dog?" The owner explained that the veterinarian had examined the pup and discovered it didn't have a hip socket. It would always be lame. The little boy became excited. "That is the little puppy that I want to buy."

The store owner said, "No, you don't have to buy that little dog. If you really want him, I'll just give him to you."

The little boy got quite upset. He pointed his finger and looked straight into the store owner's eyes. "I don't want you to give him to me. That little dog is worth every bit as much as all the other dogs, and I'll pay full price. In fact, I'll give you $2.37 now and 50 cents a month until I have him paid for."

The store owner countered, "You really don't want to buy this little dog. He is never going to run and jump and play with you like the other puppies."

At this, the little boy reached down and rolled up his pant leg to reveal a badly twisted, crippled left leg supported by a big metal brace. He looked up at the store owner and softly replied, "Well, I don't run so well myself, and the little puppy will need someone who understands."

The problem is that many men have difficulty with being sensitive. In a Western context, sensitivity is a trait viewed as less than manly, hence the saying "real men don't show emotion." Sensitivity is perceived as a threat to the male gender role, and men believe that people who are sensitive get taken advantage of. Often the mind-set goes like this: "Don't get caught up in the warm and fuzzy stuff— accomplish the task; reach the goal."

It should be stressed, however, that sensitivity is not

about being a "yes-man," being ignored, or being walked on. It is not about being a mushy, sentimental, or touchy person with no direction and conviction. Quite the opposite, being sensitive has to do with having convictions, with compassion and strength, with warmth. Sensitivity refines. The more you have of it, the better off you are.

In many places, sensitivity is beginning to be understood as the answer to problems and stresses in the workplace and in the home. It keeps us in tune with the diverse needs and conditions of those around us, and it adds to the quality of life.

Sensitivity will do a lot of good for men if they will show it. It will:

First, keep them in tune with the needs of those around them. Sensitivity nurtures understanding.

Second, make them accessible to their loved ones, friends, and those who work with them. Sensitivity facilitates flexibility.

Third, enable them to be better communicators. Sensitivity provides for true listening, the prerequisite to communication.

Fourth, allow the changes of life to take place more naturally and with less stress. Sensitivity allows opportunity to accept the vulnerabilities of life and to profit from them.

Paths to sensitivity

It's one thing to list the benefits of being sensitive; it's another thing to practice it. "In the Lord's plan human beings have been made necessary to one another. If all would do their utmost to help those who need their help, their unselfish sympathy and love, what a blessed work might be done."*

Here are four paths to achieving a deeper level of sensitivity.

Look: What is happening around you? What are the conditions, the needs? A sensitive person wants to be uplifting. He wants to help, not hurt. He wants to build, not destroy. "A cheerful look brings joy to the heart, and good news gives health to the bones" (Proverbs 15:30).

Listen: So often we know the answer and are quick to share it with the person, even before they tell us what the problem is. Sensitivity says that we deliberately keep our mouth closed and listen. The feelings inside will influence our verbal and nonverbal response. "Let the wise listen and add to their learning" (Proverbs 1:5).

Love: Love is the most important part of being sensitive. We must think love when dealing with people. We must find ways to affirm, build, and facilitate growth. Organizations and institutions across the world are beginning to realize that people are happier, more content, and more productive if they are appreciated. And that is what love is all about. "Let love and faithfulness never leave you; bind them around your neck, write them on the tablet of your heart" (Proverbs 3:3). "Hatred stirs up dissension, but love covers over all wrongs" (Proverbs 10:12).

While sensitivity is a good and effective way to live and interact with others, it is also a way that has challenges and fears. In spite of this, will you choose to be sensitive? Will you choose the path to love and growth?

* Ellen G. White, *Mind, Character, and Personality* (Nashville, Tenn.: Southern Publishing Association, 1977), 2:431.

Delbert W. Baker is an administrator and professor at Loma Linda University. He has been an editor, pastor, and counselor and has written four books. His hobbies include mountain climbing, running marathons, and collecting world currency. He is married to Susan Baker, a registered physical therapist. The Bakers have three sons.

The Stewardship of Power

by Caleb Rosado

One Memorial Day, I took my children over to Buchanan, Michigan, to watch the National Championship Mud Bog. It was the first time I had ever seen such an event. The course is a 300-foot-long pit, with mud three to four feet deep. The farther down the course, the sloppier the pit becomes and the more difficult to negotiate. The purpose of the contest was to see which competing four-wheel-drive vehicle could get through the mud bog in the fastest time.

Four different classes of vehicles were in the competition: two stock classes with different-size tires (your average street four-wheel drive truck or Jeep), one modified class, and the open class, where anything went. Most of the vehicles in the first two classes got stuck within 150 feet. In the modified class, some pushed past 200 feet, but very few. In the open class—the most exciting to watch—a number of vehicles, depending on the driver's experience, were able to get all the way through the bog.

The vehicles in the supermodified open class were awesome to behold. We were told that these open-class vehicles had such powerful engines that they were able to develop a brake horse power of 1,400, capable of hurling them through the bog at approximately eighty miles per hour. Now that's power! Such power allowed one vehicle, called "The Great White Hope" (interesting name when you connect it with the amount of power displayed), to hurl through that 300-foot mud bog in 5.6 seconds with the two front wheels off the ground. The man and machine were literally flying, and so was the mud.

When the crowd settled back down and my adrenalin flow eased a bit, I thought of other displays of power I had experienced or seen: the thrilling tractor pulls at the county fair, the thunderous thrust of the space shuttle rockets, the Z-Force roller coaster at Great America. Americans, it seems to me, have a powerful obsession with power and its display.

The definition of power

What is power? And what drives people to seek it? Power, in its essence, is the capacity to act. It manifests itself in two forms. The first is *power as coercion*—the capacity to act in a manner that influences the behavior of others even against their wishes. Based on this understanding of power, Lord Acton declared his now-famous statement: "Power tends to corrupt, absolute power corrupts absolutely."

Then there is *power as choice*—the capacity to act in a

manner that influences the behavior of others without violating free moral choice. These types of power are different in their manifestation as well as in outcome.

The stewardship of power

In Matthew 24:45-51, Jesus talks about the use and abuse of power in the story of one servant but two behaviors. The servant in this parable is entrusted with an assignment, the stewardship of power. If he is faithful in overseeing his master's household, he will be rewarded. However, if he begins to behave arbitrarily, beating his fellow servants, his reward will be very different. Harvard theologian Harvey Cox declares: "Entirely too much has been said in most churches about the stewardship of money and too little about the stewardship of power." I believe he is right.

All of us possess social power, the capacity to control the behavior of others, directly or indirectly. Even the infant in arms. When children want something and they know it is going to be tough to get, they have been around long enough to know just how to approach you: with smiles, with warmth, with tails wagging just like a puppy dog (maybe that's where they learned it, watching the dog). They come up to you very cuddly, cooing, giving you kisses and then use the warmest terms of endearment possible. Daaaaddy!

You know something? They get it most of the time. I'm a sucker for it. And the interesting thing is that I know what they are doing. And I can tell you ahead of time exactly what they are going to do and how they are going to do it, and I still fall for it. Which raises questions more about me than about them.

That's power! We call it manipulation. Nevertheless, they have gotten what they wanted, even against our wishes. Of course, it doesn't work every time. No one is that successful. But it works often enough to give them a sense of confidence in themselves and in their abilities to relate to others.

These two types of power are operative in the world today—power that operates out of selfish interest and power that operates out of selfless interest. Both have held sway throughout the history of the world. When selfish power has been on the throne, the world has been thrown in chaos. Think of the Spanish Inquisition, the Third Reich, and present forms of "ethnic cleansing." When selfless power has been wielded, the course of history has been altered. Think of Gandhi, Martin Luther King, and Mother Teresa.

The most prevalent form of power displayed in the world today—between governments, in national and city politics, in racial conflict, sometimes even in the church and in the home—is the manipulative, coercive, selfish type of power, which seeks to get its own way even against the resistance of others. Such manifestation of power derives from Satan.

God does not operate that way. God does not use force. He does not impose His will against our resistance. He does not violate our free moral choice. He operates with the second form of power, power as choice—the capacity to act in a manner that influences the behavior of others without violating free moral choice. How does God do it? Through love. Therefore, from the divine perspective, love is power.

In the parable in Matthew, selfless power and selfish power are described in terms of two words, *faithful* and *unfaithful*. One servant in the parable, but two behaviors. One operates out of love. The focus of this behavior is on the needs of others, with compassion and caring love. This is the basis of divine power—the ability to influence the behavior of others without violating their right to free choice. However, the same servant can find himself manifesting an opposite form of behavior and power, one which operates out of selfishness. The focus of the behavior here is not others but self and greed.

As men, we must not only speak of the stewardship—the management—of money, but even more important, the management of power within our homes and in our jobs. This "speaking" best "talks" through our actions, not just words. Our "walk"—how we treat our spouse, our children, our fellow employees—speaks louder than our "talk."

Conclusion

Harvey Cox tells us: "The modern equivalent of repentance is the responsible use of power." I believe there is some truth in this. There needs to be repentance in the church and in the home for the misuse of power. There must be repentance in our individual lives for the lusting after power, not in service to others, but in service to self.

Yes, there is no question that Americans have an obsession with power. But so do most human beings from all nations. The Christian, the one who is truly Christlike, must also be obsessed with power, but the right kind of power, the power of unselfish service, governed by love. It is of such a person that Ellen White declares: "The strongest argument in favor of the gospel is a loving and lovable Christian."* Why? Because love is power!

* Ellen G. White, *The Ministry of Healing*, 470.

Caleb Rosado is a professor of sociology at Humboldt State University in California.

Tears can mean vastly different things—sorrow, joy, or the fact that you've just cut up an onion. They usually indicate that something important is happening inside.

———

Boys Don't Cry

by Gary Krause

Tears and men don't mix in our society. We all know that boys don't cry. Crying betrays weakness, femininity, and cowardice. Real men conceal any feelings of weakness or vulnerability.

In his book *The Liberated Man*, Warren Farrell suggests a satirical Ten Commandments for modern men. The first commandment is: "Thou shalt not cry or expose other feelings of emotion, fear, weakness, sympathy, empathy, or involvement before thy neighbor."[1]

This attitude denies an important part of being human. Artificially blocking off tears prevents a God-given healing mechanism. This is true even at the physical level. Scientists have recently found that emotional tears (not tears caused by eye irritation) contain endorphins—wonderful chemicals that help us through stressful, painful times.

POWER FOR EVERYDAY HEROES

In his book *Resurrection,* Tolstoy describes a pitiful group of convicts who were marching to the train station in Moscow to be deported to Siberia. At one road crossing, the marching prisoners held up an elegant open carriage. Inside the carriage, a well-dressed husband and wife sat impatient at the delay in progress to their luxury country house.

Sitting opposite were their children—a little girl and a boy of eight. The father angrily scolded the driver for not crossing earlier. But all the while, the little boy was staring intently at the prisoners, horrified at their suffering, "and he tried harder and harder not to cry, supposing that it was shameful to cry on such occasions."

The little boy saw with the compassionate eyes of Jesus, but cultural pressures stifled his response. It doesn't take long for boys to learn that it's wrong to cry and that they should bottle up their emotions and maintain a brave face.

Jesus was not ashamed to cry. "Jesus wept" (John 11:35) may be the shortest text in the Bible, but it's also one of the most powerful. Jesus was no stoic. He was a living, breathing, compassionate Man who felt the pain of losing His close friend Lazarus. The appropriate response was sorrow and tears.

The Old Testament is awash with tears. Among the great weepers are Jacob (Genesis 29:11, etc.), Jonathan and David (1 Samuel 20:41), Saul (1 Samuel 24:16), Elisha (2 Kings 8:11), and Nehemiah (Nehemiah 1:4). The Old Testament is refreshingly human and honest about emotions. As the wise man said, there's "a time to weep and a time to laugh" (Ecclesiastes 3:4).

The prophet Jeremiah exclaimed, "Oh, that my head were a spring of water and my eyes a fountain of tears! I would weep day and night for the slain of my people" (Jeremiah 9:1). He despaired at his people becoming hardened and alienated from the feelings of others. You can hear the tears in his voice as he laments his people's lack of sensitivity and compassion, their greed and materialism. "Are they ashamed of their loathsome conduct?" he asks. "No, they have no shame at all; they do not even know how to blush" (Jeremiah 6:15).

Are we in danger of choking our emotional responses? Do we deny our God-given sensitivity in order to conform?

Brendan Manning tells the story of a twenty-seven-year-old man who had been born and raised a Christian but was now a recovering alcoholic with six marriages behind him. In desperation, he asked Manning to help him return to the church.

Manning says that normally he would have assured the young man that Jesus welcomed home the lost sheep and would have outlined to him the formal procedures for rejoining the church. But this time, he looked beyond the technical problem and saw a child of God who was broken and alienated.

It would have been easy for Manning to distance himself from the young man by repeating the pat phrases, feeding him the orthodox lines, and refusing to become emotionally involved. Instead, he made himself vulnerable. Tears rolled down his face as he reached out, embraced the young man, and held him for a long time. Then he said, "I have a word for you from your brother

Jesus: Welcome home."

Years of pain and rebellion had condensed into a river of tears running down the young man's cheeks, and he blurted out, "Tell me who Jesus is."

As Manning told him his own story and how Jesus had met his need, they prayed together. The young man accepted Jesus and found peace for his life.[2]

How different it would have been if Manning had decided not to open himself up to the desperate young man. It wasn't a case of being a Sensitive New Age Guy. It was a case of allowing God to operate on a real level.

It's easy to put up barriers that stop the love of Jesus Christ from touching us—every part of us. It's easy to fall into the trap of turning religion into a set of ideas and concepts for our heads, not our hearts.

"The word of God is alive and potent, beyond any sword that cuts both ways," says the writer to the Hebrews, "slicing deep to the place where mind and emotions meet, to that which holds the personality together and feeds it, and tells us what the truth is about our deepest passions and thoughts" (Hebrews 4:12, Blaiklock's translation).

You can't find any place deeper than that. We tend to hide it away, but it's the part where Jesus wants to work. He's not interested in intellectual games. We desperately need His love to shine into the place "where mind and emotions meet." We need His love to deal with "our deepest passions and thoughts." We need His love to slice deep into our lives.

How many more times will we refuse to cry?

Boys Don't Cry

1. Warren Farrell, quoted in Ronald Conway, *The End of Stupor? Australia Towards the Third Millennium* (South Melbourne: Sun Books, 1984), 59.
2. Brendan Manning, *The Signature of Jesus on the Pages of Our Lives* (Portland, Oreg.: Multnomah Press, 1992).

Gary Krause is creative director at the South Pacific Division Adventist Media Center, Sydney, Australia. He is married to Bettina, who is a law student and freelance writer.

You've looked forward to retirement so you could golf and play
tennis. The only problem is that now you don't feel like playing.
A must-read satire for those who are facing the inevitable.

———

We Grow Old—
Gracefully or Otherwise

by Claude Williams

The people of this country, men as well as women, spend
a great deal of time and money in a futile attempt to stave off
the encroachment of old age. For most of us, the steadily
advancing years seem to offer little but declining vigor, an
assortment of ills and pains, and fears for the present in
addition to those for the future. Though it may seem unlikely to some, there are worse things than growing old.
Not many, but some.

According to the legend, when Aurora asked Jupiter to
confer the gift of immortality on Tithonus, for whom she
cared greatly, if temporarily, she neglected to request eternal youth as well as eternal life. After so long a time, the
youthful goddess tired of her old lover. What to do? He was
immortal, remember, so she was stuck with him.

But Aurora, goddess of the dawn, always got up ahead of
the roosters. She had plenty of time to ponder the problem.

At length, she hit upon a tidy solution. She changed him into a grasshopper!

Old age creates quite a few problems for most of us, though being turned into a grasshopper isn't one of them. Believe it or not, some good things come with old age. After retirement, you have time to do all the things you used to just dream of doing. Retirement is wonderful. You can play golf or tennis, swim or hike. The catch, of course, is that now your bones (your muscles beat you into retirement) protest every time you do any of these things. But at least you have time for them. Most of us just can't do them.

And when you reach the age that the cashier at the drugstore does not need to ask if you are eligible for the senior citizens' discount, the bank also holds out a special favor. It's called free checking. Sooner or later, though, you discover that the checking isn't really free at all; you still have to put money into the bank before you can take money out of the bank—the same as before you got old.

Perhaps the greatest blessing of growing old is that you no longer have to get up early and go to work. Actually, you still have to work; you just don't get any pay for it. There are more little jobs lurking around the house than you ever suspected. They have been lying in ambush there ever since your first day on your first job. They have been waiting patiently ever since so that you would have something to do when you retired.

No, the rose garden of old-age retirement is not free of thorns. The brain can wither and dry up along with the muscle tone and skin. The way to avoid this unfortunate situation is to use the brain. In old age, it is easier than using muscle. Read. Talk to people who have something interesting, perhaps even important, to say.

An easy but rewarding armchair exercise is working crossword puzzles. You will acquire a marvelous new vocabulary that will require a really agile brain to work into any conversation.

For any person, including the often-envied young, it is important to spend time every day with your books, your music, your pets, your family, and your friends. All these are conducive to mental health and happiness; and these, in turn, are conducive to physical health.

But most important of all is spending time daily with your heavenly Father. No amount of time spent in other ways will ever lead anywhere worth going, unless He directs your steps.

I'm looking forward to that day when "the trumpet shall sound, . . . and we shall be changed." When "this mortal must put on immortality" (1 Corinthians 15:52, 53, KJV). There will be no dry, wrinkly skin when Jesus comes. No rheumatism, no arthritis, no faltering steps.

I'm going to a land where I'll never grow old!

Claude Williams is a retired teacher living in Sallis, Mississippi.

You were created to be a blessing—
not just leave behind a blessing.

———

Divine Manpower

by Salim Hasbani

David spent a lifetime seeking his father's approval. His father wanted him to be the best and the brightest. And David tried–how he tried; but he was never able to live up to his father's expectations. When his father lay dying, David flew across the country to be by his bedside and plead one last time, "Please say you love me, please." David's words trailed off into tears as he leaned over the now-still form of his father.

Perhaps you know someone like David. Maybe you've walked in his shoes. What is it in a person's makeup that makes him desperately need what the Bible calls "the father's blessing"?

An old man by the name of Isaac was dying. His eyesight had failed him. He knew deep in his heart that his days were numbered. Yet he could not die until he had performed an important cultural and spiritual task that had come down to him through many generations.

As Jacob stood outside his father's tent, he realized that by deceiving his father and pretending to be the older son, Esau, he would illegally receive the blessing that he desperately wanted. After a while, Esau entered his father's tent. He was devastated to discover that the blessing had been passed on to his brother. He cried in agony, "Bless me, even me also, O my father" (Genesis 27:34, KJV). What was this blessing that both men coveted?

When God created man, you and I included, He endowed him with great power. Power that can be used to reflect God's own image and glory in a mighty way, to bless his wife, his sons, his daughters. For to them, the father and the husband is to be a living model of what God is like. To love, to cherish, to uphold, and to restore in them the great value God intended for His sons and daughters to have, so that they, in turn, could reflect the divine glory.

Man at work, by the very nature of his job and his personality makeup, is usually on the fast track: making tough decisions, seeking promotion, being competitive, earning money to support his family, improving efficiencies, and pleasing the demanding boss. It is very difficult for this cold, tired, efficient "machine" to transform himself on demand into a loving, doting father and a caring, understanding husband as soon as he crosses the threshold of his home.

Unfortunately, in most cases, this same cold, harsh work-related use of personal power is carried home after working hours and is used by man to abuse and destroy those who love him and those he loves the most.

What complicates matters is that these caring attributes are easy to express. But men in our society are expected to portray a tough image. Shedding tears of sympathy, joy, or sadness by men is considered a weakness.

So what is the solution? Is it perhaps that man needs to manage his great God-given power? This trait has to be learned and developed. As in many character-modification and life-altering changes, a higher power is needed to affect changes in our personalties—the power of the Holy Spirit.

God gave value and power to man when He created him in His image. The Bible teaches us that God's glory is His character, and His character is revealed in His law. Through Him, we can acquire the character of God, to fashion our intellect and feelings. That is how a man passes on the blessings to his family.

To describe man's personal power is to describe his character, reflected in such words as *empathy, caring, compassion, dependability, commitment,* and *self-sacrificing love.*

For many years, men have been portrayed by television and dinner speakers as dense, unromantic, uncaring, evil, and violent. Satan, in his attack on God's creation and on the family, has managed to convince our world that consistent love and unwavering commitment are not important. Thus he has trivialized God's assigned role for man as the priest of the home.

To follow Jesus is to reflect His character. To uphold his wife, children, neighbors, and co-workers. No greater gift can a father offer his children than the legacy of loving their mother. No greater tribute can a husband bestow upon his wife than to model himself after Christ's example and show his children what God is like. To use the great personal power God has given him to love and to cherish others for all eternity.

Through the pen of inspiration, Paul the apostle sent the Ephesian church a job description for a husband: to be the head of the wife, as Jesus is the head of the church. Jesus loved the church and laid down His own life for it so the church could have eternal life. Husbands are admonished to love their wives as their own body (see Ephesians 5:22-31).

The greatest gift that a father can give his family is his time, his understanding, his affirmation, his acceptance, and his lifelong commitment. To use our God-given power is to value, to protect, and to cherish those whom we love as God loves us.

"Behold, what manner of love the Father hath bestowed upon us, that we should be called the sons of God" (1 John 3:1, KJV). What a value this places upon man! And what a great responsibility for every man to pass on.

Salim Hasbani was born in Beirut, Lebanon. He received his Bachelor of Arts degree in business administration from Middle East College in Beirut. He served as mission treasurer in several mission fields in the Middle East Union. He is presently employed by a government hospital in Bakersfield, California, as hospital controller. Mr. Hasbani has formed ministries for men in his area.

His girlfriend slipped him the answers to all the quizzes, but one wise teacher chose to remain silent and taught him a valuable lesson on human behavior that surpassed the textbooks.

————

I Knew You
Weren't a Cheater

by M. Jerry Davis

Mr. Shepherd was one of my seventh-grade teachers. One of the best—math, health, and physical education. He didn't teach school, he taught people. He was about five-foot-six. Many of us were as tall or taller than he, yet we all looked up to him. He was balding and had the paunch of a penguin. I never wondered how old he was. The atmosphere of his classroom was easy, respectful, never uptight.

It was Mr. Shepherd who organized the Friday-afternoon games and Sunday-afternoon sports so dads could play as well. When he saw that some of us were getting interested in girls, he had a dinner at his house at which we could learn to interact. We learned square roots and the names of bones and, I now realize, a whole lot more.

Still, a dark shadow fell across our time together. Bonnie was in the eighth grade. I was sweet on her. She had health class just before I did. As we passed in the hall, she would slip me a sheet with the answers to the quiz. I cheated my way through the class. I felt bad, and when the year was over, I determined never to cheat again. There was no overwhelming guilt. It simply rested in the recesses of my memory—until . . .

I was a high-school junior. English was my favorite class. I happened, one day, to glance at the window. The lower panes were opaque, the upper clear. A man's head bobbed by, visible only from the top of ears—Mr. Shepherd.

Without permission, I raced out of the classroom and caught up to Mr. Shepherd as he got into his car.

"Mr. Shepherd," I said.

"Jerry," he remembered.

"I have something to tell you," I stammered. "When I was in your health class, in the seventh grade, I cheated."

"I know you did."

I was surprised into silence.

He continued, "But I knew you weren't a cheater, and I didn't want to embarrass you needlessly."

I knew then why I had always felt cared for by Mr. Shepherd, and I determined to remember that people are more than their behavior, greater than their performance, and grander than their foolishness.

Jerry Davis was born in Walla Walla, Washington. He attended La Sierra College, Andrews University, and the School of Theology at Claremont. He has served as chaplain at Loma Linda University Medical Center since 1970 and is also supervisor for the Association for Clinical Pastoral Education.

An Ode to Creation

by Joe Crews

Once upon a time in the long, long ago,
There was no one to talk to, and no place to go.
No man had been created, and no woman made;
The earth's verdant carpet had not yet been laid.
If someone had been there to view the strange sight,
He would have seen nothing, for there was no light.
Imagine the heavens without any stars;
No sunrise or sunsets; no Venus, no Mars.
The spot where our planet now hangs in its place
Was totally empty, surrounded by space.

God had no material to shape into worlds,
No human genetics to make boys and girls.
But the absence of matter was nothing to God,
His word gave existence to rock, soil, and clod.
The world came together; each atom and quark,

POWER FOR EVERYDAY HEROES

Though filled with confusion, and utterly dark.
Then out of the void of that infinite night
A firm voice commanded, "Let there be light."
The darkness fell back like a demon retreating,
And the glory of noonday from God was proceeding.
The substance which sprang from that first day of time
Was covered with water though still in its prime.

On day number two God spoke once again,
And the heavens were lifted to form a great span.
The waters divided, above and below,
But land still was covered, and nothing could grow.
The third day brought changes of global design;
The oceans were measured, and God drew a line,
Dividing the waters from mountain and plain,
Establishing boundaries for each to maintain.
But the planet was somber and colorless too.
The ground had no cover, and the sky was not blue.

So then came an action that was unique to God.
He spoke to the earth that it should bring forth its sod.
No creatures were present to witness that scene,
But earth's ugly surface transformed into green.
The grasses, the fruit trees, and flowers without end
Covered the landscape with delicate blend.
No picture of nature by man's finest art
Can equal the glory, or make the least start,
Of showing how perfect the earth then was made,
When that carpet of verdure by God's hand was laid.
Thus ended the third day with its colors and tints,

An Ode to Creation

As the air filled with fragrance and sweet-smelling scents.

Then God took away all the mist and the haze
And did something special for the nights and the days.
He placed in the heavens great luminous lights,
The sun ruling daytime; the moon ruling nights.
But God didn't set them to switch on and off,
The sunset was peaceful, and twilight was soft.
Slowly the colors grew dim in the west,
As velvety shadows, at God's own behest,
Gave way to the evening, of the fourth day of time,
While stars made their debut in glory sublime.

But no one was present to see or to feel,
No eyes to which beauty could make its appeal.
Inanimate nature lay silent and still;
Not a sound; not a rustle, from valley or hill.
By the side of the ocean, it was not quite the same.
There was lapping and splashing, though gentle and tame.
But no gulls were crying, and no sand crabs played,
No creature exited; no fish had been made.
So the Creator moved, as the fifth day began,
To fill all the waters, by His infinite plan,
With sharks and sea horses, with salmon and seals,
With strange-looking coral and plankton and eels.
Then God made the birds, on the very same day,
Some with bright plumage, and some a dull gray.
But all had a function, regardless of size,
And each moved by instinct, incredibly wise
In migrating, nesting, or teaching their young

POWER FOR EVERYDAY HEROES

To find their own dinner, by beak or by tongue.

On day number six it was easy to see,
The plants couldn't flourish, with no honey bee.
So God made the insects, the bugs and the beasts
And all the *great* creatures as well as the least.
The elephant family, the tiger and deer;
Some looked majestic and others looked queer.
Zebras, gorillas, and species galore,
But none were ferocious in spite of their roar.
They mingled together in fearless accord,
None tried to threaten or make himself lord.
Each male had a female; God made them a pair.
For each a companion with whom it could share.
God told every creature that they should give birth,
"Multiply quickly and fill all the earth."

But something was missing amidst all the life.
Though nature was peaceful, and no one in strife,
The Maker was lonely for those who could choose
Freely to serve Him or freely refuse.
So in His omniscience God worked out a plan
To form a new creature—a species called man.
For this undertaking God chose a strange tack.
Instead of commanding, He bent His own back,
And carefully molded a body of clay,
So totally Godlike in every small way.
The Master was pleased with His perfect design.
"The image," He said, "is exactly like mine."
So into his nostrils God breathed His own breath,

An Ode to Creation

And Adam awakened as though from a death.

It must have felt strange to be thrust into being.
He doubtless was thrilled by his hearing and seeing,
But God had a job for His new counterpart.
In his first day of life God told him to start
And name all the creatures, from rhinos to bears.
So Adam looked close as they passed by in pairs,
And gave each a name that would match its physique,
From the pig with its snout to the bird with it beak.

Now Adam was ruler of all living things,
His realm more expansive than monarchs or kings.
But all of his subjects were creature or bird,
Some hairy, some feathered, and some richly furred.
He longed for a helpmeet of his very kind;
Among all the creatures, not one could he find.

Aware of man's hunger for someone to love,
God moved with compassion, as He watched from above.
And then He devised something special and new.
A female companion, which the Creator drew
From Adam's own body, right next to his heart,
So the two, joined together, would nevermore part.

When Adam awoke from the sleep God induced,
He had no awareness that his ribs were reduced.
His total attention was focused on Eve.
So lovely a being he could not conceive.
She was bone of his body and they twain were one,

POWER FOR EVERYDAY HEROES

To cleave to each other till life should be done.

So harmony reigned from the east to the west.
God said it was good, and now He would rest.
On the seventh day Sabbath no work would be done.
That time would be holy from setting of sun,
A lasting reminder that He made the earth,
And to worship the Maker who brought it to birth.

For six thousand years that command has been given,
And for much of that time it was broken and riven.
But the words of that law have been etched in the heart
Of the heirs of salvation, who will play a great part
In restoring the Sabbath to its own rightful place.
And soon when He comes and we meet face to face,
Jesus will create a world without sin,
And we will dwell with Him—world without end.

Joe Crews graduated from Andrews University with his master's degree in systematic theology. Besides pastoring, he spent five years overseas in Pakistan and India as a missionary. He is best remembered as the founder of *Amazing Facts* radio and television ministry. He wrote this poem shortly before his death in 1994.

Marvin seemed to be a hopeless cause. He drank. He cursed.
Refused to attend church. But one little girl's faith was
rewarded when she refused to give up on her daddy.

———

With God, All Things
Are Possible

by Bill May

With man this is impossible, but with God all things are
possible (Matthew 19:26).

Early in our ministry, my wife and I were sent to Carlsbad,
New Mexico. The church there consisted of one woman
who was baptized through the *Voice of Prophecy* and one
family who kept their business open on Sabbath and weren't
too strong in the Lord.

Shortly after we arrived in Carlsbad, the district pastor and
I conducted an evangelistic series. When it was over, the
church had seven members—including my wife and me.

One Sabbath morning I stood up to preach and noticed a
little girl sitting on the front row. She appeared to be about
seven years old. I thought to myself, *Oh no*, because she was all
by herself, and when little ones are in church by themselves,
the sermon seems so long, and all sorts of things can happen.
I remember one time a little girl lay down on the front seat,

177

stuck her leg up in the air, and started waving it around. Another time I'd had little children in the front row turn around and make faces at the people while I preached. That's pretty hard to compete with!

So when I spotted the little girl alone, I groaned. *This is all I need*. But I could have forgotten about that, because this particular little girl wasn't like that at all. When I started speaking, she glued her eyes on me and sat quietly through the whole sermon. Later, I learned that her name was Jan and a member had invited her because her parents didn't attend any church.

Not long after that, we had a special Sabbath on which we asked everyone to commit to leading one person to Jesus in a year. We promised to help them find someone to work with if they would agree to lead one person to Jesus. We gave them a couple of weeks to think about it, and then in my sermon I spoke about what God can do through us. I explained that whether or not we feel qualified is irrelevant—we just need to go out and start sharing with people how good the Lord is. And at the close I said, "Now I know you've had time to think about this, and I'm asking you to commit by standing." As I looked around, everyone was just sitting there—except this one little girl, Jan. She literally leapt to her feet and stood as tall as she could! The whole congregation smiled, and soon everyone stood.

At the door after the service, Jan asked me, "Did you see me stand?"

And I said, "Yes, I surely did! It was fabulous; it was an inspiration to all of us."

Then she said, "I've got to talk to you about that. I think I did it wrong."

I said, "No, I don't think so. It looked fine to me."

But she persisted. "Didn't you say that we should stand if we wanted to lead one soul to Jesus?" When I answered Yes, she said, "Well, that's why I think I might not have done it right. I want to win two souls—my mother and my father. Is that all right?"

"Oh yes," I assured her. "That's even better."

Jan went home and started working on her parents. In about five weeks, her mother came to church, and she never missed another Sabbath. Her father, though, was something else. Marvin was one of the nicest guys in the world, but he had no interest at all in the things of God.

I should tell you that I went to see Jan's mother before she started attending church. I met her at the door and introduced myself, and she said, "Come in this house!" So I went in, and we sat down.

I told her, "We're so glad your little daughter has been coming to church."

And she said, "Yes, she really likes it."

We talked about ten or fifteen minutes, and then I said, "You know, there's just one little thing that's not quite perfect about your daughter coming to church."

She said, "Oh, what's that?"

Smiling, I replied, "She comes without her mother."

"Oh," she said slowly. "We're just not church people. Besides, I don't think I need to, because Jan comes home and preaches me the sermon. I can tell you everything you preached last week." And she proceeded to give me an outline of the sermon!

After Jan's mother had been attending church for some

time, I decided to get acquainted with her father. So I went to their house one day while everyone else was gone and talked to Marvin. I invited him to come to church. Then the strangest thing happened. I've never had anything like it happen before or since. Marvin started laughing—and I don't mean a little laugh. He leaned back in his chair and started roaring with laughter. To him, that was the most preposterous thing anybody could have said.

Pretty soon, the whole church was praying for Marvin. The members got to know him because he would come to every one of our church socials. But if some well-meaning church member would start talking to him about religious things, Marvin would leave as fast as he could.

In spite of his stubbornness, Jan never gave up on her daddy. Years later, Marvin himself told me the whole story. He said that one Sabbath he'd been in town when his wife and daughter came home from church. When they had sat down to eat, Jan said, "Daddy, over at the church they told us that you ought to pray before you eat. Can we do that?"

And he'd said, "No, I don't know how to pray. You can forget that idea!"

Jan said, "No, I don't mean that. I mean, can I do it? Would you let me pray?"

Marvin said he looked at his little girl, and she looked so sincere. He figured it couldn't hurt, so he said, "Yeah, I guess it's all right." (Later, he said, "Little did I know what I was getting into!")

Anyway, Jan stood at the head of the table and thanked God for the food. Marvin was watching her the whole time—he never closed his eyes. He was thinking, *Come on, let's get this thing over with*, when she said, "Now, Lord, we've got a problem at this house, and it's my daddy. He won't go to church, and he won't keep the Sabbath. . . ." She went right on down the line, naming her daddy's "problems."

Marvin said his first thought was to leap out of his chair and yell, "Cut that out!" but somehow he couldn't. Her prayer affected him so deeply that he had to get up and tiptoe out of the room and down the hall to the bathroom. When he had closed the door, he began to bawl like a baby—but he didn't want Jan to know that! So he waited until he had regained his composure, then washed his face and returned to the table.

By that time, the prayer was over. Jan looked at him as if to say, "Boy, you are a tough case! You even walk out during prayer!" But she kept working on him, and soon the whole church began to see the results of her efforts.

One Sabbath just before I was to step onto the platform, I decided to open the side door a crack to see who was out in the congregation. As I was looking out, the door to the church opened, and in walked Marvin. The church was fairly full, and Marvin had to walk down to the front and sit down beside a great big fellow who had been a wrestler and had worked in the mines.

So there was Marvin, sitting next to this big, tough fellow whose nose had been knocked off to one side in some encounter. My sermon wasn't one geared to a call, but while I was preaching, I just happened to notice that tears were streaming down Marvin's face. He looked so uncomfortable, and I could tell he was thinking, *What in the world am I here for? I don't believe any of this, and here I'm sitting in this church bawling, and that makes me so upset.*

It was obvious he was shaken up and didn't know what to do. Pretty soon, Marvin reached over and got a hymnbook and held it up so the big guy couldn't see him crying. I'll never forget that ex-wrestler looking at that book and wondering what in the world Marvin was doing!

Marvin soon regained his composure and put the book down. But during the closing hymn, Marvin was holding onto the hymnal with the wrestler when he began to cry again. Marvin really didn't know what to do that time, because he knew he needed the book that the other man was holding onto! Finally, Marvin was so miserable that he just jerked the book out of the man's hand and held it up between them.

After the closing prayer, Marvin tore out of that building. I ran after him and caught him just as he was getting into his pickup truck. I said, "Marvin, the Lord spoke to you, didn't He?"

And Marvin snapped, "No."

"Marvin, you don't have to listen to me, and you don't have to listen to your wife, and you don't have to listen to Jan. But if God speaks, you've got to listen."

At that point, Marvin jerked his arm back and growled, "I told you—nobody spoke to me!" He started the pickup and had it wide open before he let out the clutch. Marvin spun out of there—the gravel was flying—and he left rubber and a cloud of smoke once he finally hit the pavement.

Wherever Marvin went, it wasn't home. Later that afternoon, his family called me and asked if I had heard from him. I hadn't. Nobody heard from him Sunday, Monday,

Tuesday, or Wednesday. But when Thursday night came and Marvin still hadn't come home, we got a bunch of the church members together. I told them, "He's God's person; he's not ours. God is watching over him."

Marvin knocked on my door Friday morning. He looked pathetic. His hair was all over the place, he hadn't shaved in a week, and his clothes were all wrinkled as if he had slept on the ground every night. He looked bad.

Marvin looked at me and said, "I came to church last week."

I said, "Yes. It was wonderful."

"I told you that God didn't speak to me, but He did. I didn't want to hear Him, so I decided to go out and get so drunk that I wouldn't remember one thing. I've done that many times. When things get tough, I just go out and get soused. Well, I went out and started drinking, and I have consumed enough liquor to float a battleship. And do you know, I have not been drunk for one single second. And the voice is still speaking to me. I want to come to the Lord, but I don't know how."

We talked for a few minutes, then I invited Marvin to kneel with me. Marvin came to the Lord that day. He served as the head elder of that church for many years, until his death just recently.

Jan was only seven years old when she decided that with God's help she could win two to the Lord. When that spirit really strikes God's people everywhere, the work will be finished quickly. God wants to use every one of us. Everyone has somebody that nobody else can reach.

May God help us to measure up to this great hour in which we live.

Remember, we have a God who can do all things.

———————————

Bill May has conducted over one hundred evangelistic campaigns. He has served in administration in two conferences and one union conference. He is the author of the Revelation Seminar lessons from *Seminars Unlimited*, and he also wrote the *Amazing Facts* information folders and the new revised and enlarged study guides.